S
WITHOUT PUTTING
ON WEIGHT

STOP SMOKING
WITHOUT PUTTING
ON WEIGHT

Penny Ross MSc PhD FRSA

Thorsons
An Imprint of HarperCollins*Publishers*

Thorsons
An Imprint of HarperCollins*Publishers*
77–85 Fulham Palace Road,
Hammersmith, London W6 8JB

Published by Thorsons 1992
1 3 5 7 9 10 8 6 4 2

A catalogue record for this book
is available from the British Library

ISBN 0 7225 2634 2

Typeset by Harper Phototypesetters Limited
Northampton, England
Printed in Great Britain by
HarperCollinsManufacturing Glasgow

CONTENTS

To the many women (and men) who are struggling to break free from the trap of smoking to be slim.

ACKNOWLEDGEMENTS

My first debt of gratitude lies with the many smokers and ex-smokers who shared with me their experiences of 'smoking to be slim'. Without them, this book could not have been written. Nor could I have put pen to paper if I had not been privileged to work over several years with dedicated colleagues, in the fields of human nutrition, and latterly, as Director of QUIT, smoking and health. It was here that I co-wrote, with Fiona Watson, the original 'Quit and Stay Slim', funded by the W & M Morris Charitable Trust. It was the success of this leaflet which provided the inspiration for this book.

It was also at QUIT that I learnt the 'nuts and bolts' of helping people to stop smoking. Our aim was to enable would-be quitters to work through their own problems and reach their own solutions; and as counsellors we did not allow our own personal experiences or beliefs to interfere. It is a valuable approach, but not without its frustrations, not the least of which is the influence of the other side, by which I mean the tobacco industry. While health professionals are helping people to reach a reasoned decision on the basis of the facts, their every step forward is being undermined by an industry which persists not only in evading them, but counteracting appropriate action with a quality of advertising and lobbying which only tobacco profits can buy. Yet we know that the majority of smokers would like to quit. A few find it really difficult and need specialist help, but the stumbling block for most is that the advantages of quitting are perceived to be outweighed by the 'disadvantages'. Faced with this, what are we to do? Many of us have personal experiences of tackling a health problem; we all know other people who have done so; and, regrettably, we are well aware of the consequences of doing otherwise. We may not be able to afford multi-million dollar advertising campaigns, but we can, from time to time, come out from behind our blank screens and take a proactive stance, and encourage people to stop smoking in the best way we know how. In my own way, that is what I have tried to do in this book.

The other problem which arises in writing for a lay audience is where to draw the line between readability and rigour. I have a scientific training and this leads me to be suspicious of simple explanations of complex problems, but if I had included every 'if', 'but', 'why' and 'wherefore', I would have bored most readers stiff. Inevitably, there has had to be compromise, but this does not mean that the book is under-researched. I would like to thank, in particular, Sandi Wilson, Director of QUIT and Amanda Sandford, information officer at ASH for access to their libraries; Professor R Klesges, University of Memphis, Tennessee, for useful information; Julia Wadsworth, Dr Tommy Carr, Dr Alison Tedstone and Dr Lesley Godfrey who read and commented on sections of the text; and Dr

Geraldine McNeill, for helpful calculations on energy balance and weight gain. I would also like to acknowledge the use of Bobbie Jacobson's excellent book *Beating the Ladykillers* (Victor Gollancz, London, 1988), on which I drew substantially in my first chapter, 'A Lucky Strike'.

Perhaps inevitably, the real burden of writing a book falls upon the author's family. My mother-in-law (no – really!) painstakingly read and commented on successive drafts of the text, and Sandra Fordham provided wonderful care for our baby son in mum's absence, as well as acting as a sounding board for new ideas. Last but not least, I would like to thank my parents, and especially my husband, for giving me the confidence and moral support which enabled me to take the task to completion.

INTRODUCTION:
CONFESSIONS OF A
FORMER SMOKER

I stopped smoking on April 3rd, 1984. It was an event in my life which has the same sort of significance as the shooting in 1963 of the American President, John F. Kennedy: years later, I can pinpoint exactly where I was and what I was doing at the time.

Not that my decision to stop smoking was a flash in the pan. What had begun as a nagging doubt was now ticking away in my mind like a time bomb. I had pains in my legs when I walked and I was worried sick about the damage that smoking was doing to my health. I hated the smell of smoke on my hair and clothes. And I longed to be free of the constant worry of whether and when I could next have a cigarette.

I had been thinking about this in the small hours, with the result that I overslept on the morning of an appointment with the doctor. Skipping my usual 'breakfast' of two cigarettes and a cup of coffee, I dressed and ran for the Underground. The doors were about to close as I reached the platform, so I jumped on to the nearest carriage, which happened to be a non-smoker (smoking on the London tubes was not completely banned for another three months).

My appointment with the doctor was routine and as usual she asked about my smoking. 'You really should stop,' she said. 'I've cut down,' I said, wishing it were true. 'Is there anything else you want to ask me about?' she continued. 'No,' I replied, wondering if I should tell her about the pains in my legs.

When I eventually reached my office it was past 11 o'clock. By now I would normally have smoked at least 5 cigarettes. It struck me that if I could just keep it up, I would have stopped. With that, I threw a half-empty packet of Dunhill into the wastepaper basket and I have never smoked since. But let me tell you how it was that I came to be smoking in the first place.

It was 1977, I was 17 and I was lamenting, not for the first time, my ever-expanding size. To say that I was unhappy about it was an understatement: I was desolate. I had tried dieting many times and lost weight, only to put it on again, and more. I was prepared to do anything to lose weight, and in the end I decided to take up smoking.

I cannot say that it really helped. Armed with my cigarettes, I went on a crash diet which I stuck to rigidly and lost weight, but three months later I was back where I started, except that I was now smoking 20 cigarettes a day. Like most people who start smoking I had assumed that I would be able to stop just as easily, but I now found this to be far from the truth.

In the January of 1978, I left the UK to spend 6 months living in the American Mid-West. It was an opportunity of a lifetime and one which I enjoyed in many ways, but I would have enjoyed it far more if I had been slimmer. Being fat meant being different, which was the last thing I wanted to be. It meant avoiding all the things which slim teenagers take for granted–like going swimming or wearing the latest jeans. I was 18 and missing out on life, and food and cigarettes were my only consolation. I returned home 15lb (7kg) heavier, a diet sheet in one hand, and 200 Kool in the other.

September marked the start of a three-year stint at University, where I found myself sharing accommodation with a group of medical students who were fiercely anti-smoking. I was the only smoker and my new friends were determined to stop me at all costs. In the end they got to me by pushing firecrackers into my cigarettes so that they blew up in my face every time I lit up. Spurred on by this humiliating (although well-intentioned) treatment, I finally decided to quit. It was difficult, but not that difficult–except that I now found without cigarettes, I couldn't stop eating.

The shock of seeing my weight rocket upwards once again served as the final blow. I joined a slimming club and started smoking again. I succeeded in losing weight, although not quite as much as I'd hoped, and this time, I managed to keep it off. But it was a tortured existence. I counted the calories in everything I ate until I knew them by heart, and I forced myself to stay within strict limits. I weighed myself at least twice a week, and registered with trepidation the slightest upward move on the dial. I was forever starting a diet on Monday, only to give up again on Tuesday or Wednesday. Cigarettes were by now my constant companion; I smoked to prevent myself eating and ate when I was prevented from smoking. I was smoking 30 cigarettes a day on a good day and sometimes as many as 60–and in more than 5 years I did not go a single day without a cigarette.

Still in search of a less painful solution to my problems, I went on to study for a further degree, in Human Nutrition. It was here that I was eventually to get to grips with things; not, I have to say, because of anything I learnt in my lectures, but because it helped me get things in perspective. Thinking about poverty and starvation made me realize that I was really one of the lucky ones. With so many children dying because they did not have enough to eat, how could I waste so much time thinking about food and dieting? Gradually I stopped worrying about my size and gave up the constant round of dieting, bingeing and dieting again. To my surprise, I did not gain weight. I lost it. I threw away my calorie chart and although much of it is still imprinted on my mind, I did manage to stop calculating the cost of every meal. I started to enjoy good food and good health. Except of course, that I was still a smoker–until, on that April day in 1984, I resolved to quit once and for all.

This time, I found it almost impossibly difficult. I was convinced that I would fall apart without cigarettes, and I was petrified that I would put on weight. In the event, both fears turned out to be unfounded. In the space of a few months I put on just 5lb (2¼kg), which I later lost without trying. My self-confidence improved and if anything I coped better than before. I no longer spent my days thinking about eating and smoking–instead I was learning to get on with life.

Still, if stopping smoking had convinced me of one thing, it was that there was not enough help available for people who wanted to quit. I had managed to find a few guides in my local bookshop, but as they were mostly about planning to stop, it was a bit late. The only glimmer of hope was a notice in my doctor's surgery which pointed me in the direction of a 'stop smoking' clinic in North London. It was a bit of a trek to get there, but I thought it might help. It did. At the clinic, I met other people who had just quit smoking, and was able to talk over my worries with them. Although I did not return to the clinic, it gave me an idea of what to do next.

Several years later, I left my job as a medical researcher and went to work for a voluntary organization called the National Society of Non Smokers. During the next three years, it was to be transformed into QUIT–the charity dedicated to helping smokers to stop. My job brought me into contact with literally thousands of would-be quitters who contacted us for advice and counselling, or joined our stop smoking groups.

I was now to discover that my experience was by no means unique. For many would-be quitters, fear of putting on weight was of paramount importance, whether they had never given a second thought to their size until now, or whether, like me, they had struggled with a weight problem for years. I read as much as I could about the subject, and I listened and learnt from the smokers and ex-smokers I met in the course of my work. Of course, every smoker is different and everyone has to find their own personal stop smoking strategy. But I am sure that if I had known in 1984 what I know now, my own task of stopping smoking would have been much less daunting.

Introduction

I have written this book for all those smokers who would like to be free of smoking, but fear putting on weight so much that they dare not quit. In writing it, my greatest wish has been that I could meet you, the reader, and talk to you about the reasons which led you to buy this book. As it is, I have had to make an educated guess. I know that there are many would-be ex-smokers for whom staying slim is not, and never has been, an issue. Some of them worry about putting on weight, perhaps because they've read that stopping smoking might make them fat, or because they know someone else who stopped smoking and put on a lot of weight. You might be one of them. My guess, though, is that you are more likely to be someone who smokes because you find it difficult to stay slim (or because you want to lose weight), or someone who has recently stopped smoking, gained weight and wants to know what to do about it. For this reason, the book is as much a guide to staying slim without smoking as a guide to stopping smoking without gaining weight.

This book does not offer a miracle cure for smoking; nor can it offer an instant solution to a long-term problem with weight or dieting. I cannot promise to make stopping smoking easy, although you may well find it much easier than you think. But I do sincerely hope that somewhere in these pages you will find the help and encouragement which will allow you to break free from the trap of smoking to be slim.

Penny Ross
June 1992

1

A LUCKY STRIKE

'Who knows, perhaps if, in *Now Voyager*, Paul Heinreid had not lit two cigarettes and passed one to Bette Davis, but instead offered her his half-licked wine gum, the whole history of modern coughing might have been different.'

Alan Coren
Keep Our Wits About You
The Times 1991 [1]

Ever since cigarettes were launched to an unsuspecting female market, we have been led to believe that smoking could make us slim.

Around the turn of this century, thanks to the availability of the new mass-produced machine-made cigarettes, tobacco became big business. The low cost and convenience of the cigarette, combined with increasing prosperity, made for an ideal time to expand the market for tobacco. By the start of the 1920s, smoking, which had hitherto been a habit practised only by a wealthy minority, had achieved popular acclaim. But it was men, rather than women, who were persuaded to take up the habit, passing up their cigars and pipes in favour of the new cheaper cigarettes. The

---

[1] Reproduced with kind permission of Alan Coren.

tobacco industry was winning; but it was winning only half the battle.

Women proved to be an altogether harder nut to crack. Although our pictures had graced the cigarette cards which had been used so successfully to sell cigarettes to men, the idea of a woman smoking herself was out of the question. Indeed, it was not until the 1920s that the tobacco industry, spurred on by women's new-found liberation, dared to promote cigarettes for women, and even then, they had a spectacular lack of success. In 1927, Marlboro, later relaunched as the macho cigarette, were marketed for ladies with red cork tips 'for ruby lips'. In the US, fashionable women were encouraged not to be coy about smoking: 'Be nonchalant – light a Murad' beckoned one advertisement, 'Blow some my way' suggested another. But women were not impressed.

Then the president of American Tobacco, the manufacturers of Lucky Strike, struck gold with an idea which was, within two years, to turn them into America's best selling brand. According to his own account:

'There was a big stout negro lady chewing on gum. And there was a taxi-cab coming the other way. I looked and there was a young lady sitting in the taxi-cab with a long cigarette holder in her mouth and her skirts were pretty high, and she had a pretty good figure . . . But right there and then it hit me; there was this colored lady that was stout and chewing and there was this young girl that was slim and smoking a cigarette'.

Thus was born the slogan: 'To keep a slender figure –

Reach for a Lucky instead of a Sweet'. And all across America, women did just that. The slogan for Lucky Strike had struck women just where it hurt. Generations of women who were already trapped by the 20th-century notion that 'to be beautiful is to be slim' were now caught in a new trap: they were to become hooked on cigarettes.

The fashion for smoking among women elsewhere owed no less to a successful marketing campaign than did the trend in the USA. Wherever and whenever cigarettes were promoted, advertisers were quick to link them with elegance, sophistication and success, images which were reinforced by the glamorous, slender film stars of the day: Lana Turner, Marlene Dietrich, Greta Garbo, Bette Davis, to name but a few; and Betty Grable, who was later to die tragically of a smoking-related disease.

That women will buy almost anything which claims to help them keep or achieve a fashionable figure has not been lost on an industry which has exploited every opportunity to link cigarettes with slimness, and slimness with success. Even when filter cigarettes were introduced, it was argued that they would have a special appeal to women because they were reminiscent of the long, slender cigarette holders which had been popularized by the flapper girls in the 1920s. Later, in the 1960s as the sexual revolution raged, came the start of international attempts to fashion an exclusively female cigarette. Here slimness was (and still is) a key attribute. Consider, for example, Virginia Slims, which are, among other things, 'Slimmer than the fat cigarettes men smoke'; Virginia

Superslims, advertised by *superslim* (grotesquely gaunt?) models; More – long, slim and brown for the 'confident, sophisticated' woman; Kim, which were 'Long, Slender, Light and Mellow;' Misty and Vogue, slim cigarettes, marketed in delicate, pastel packaging; and Silva Thins, audaciously promoted to British smokers as a slimming aid, albeit with limited success. Even cigarette lighters were subjected to sexual discrimination. While men sported macho lighters encased in buffalo hide, the girls apparently loved the Ronson Milady – a lighter of petite dimensions, fashioned for 'girls of all sizes'.

Meanwhile, the wheel has gone full circle. Albert Lasker, the American ad man who coined the successful Lucky Strike slogan, left the tobacco industry behind him and helped to set up the American Cancer Society. Janet Sackman, the carefree model girl who featured in advertisements for Lucky Strike, had cancer of the larynx, and has devoted the rest of her life to campaigning against tobacco promotion. Sadly, many of those who are helped by their efforts would have no need of them if they had not been persuaded to smoke in the first place.

But the legacy lives on. You are not alone if you believe that smoking helps you to slim or to stay slim. In 1982, a survey of over 1000 German patients found that the (supposed) weight control effects of smoking were highly valued among smokers, especially women. In another more recent study, almost one in three American college students who smoked reported using their smoking to control their weight, while one in five women who had tried to quit smoking, but failed, attributed their relapse to weight gain. And that's not all. Fear of weight gain seems to be an important reason why some smokers have never even *tried* to quit.

Perhaps even more distressing is that fear of fatness is one of the things which influences the decisions that tomorrow's smokers, our children, make about whether to start or continue smoking. When a group of schoolchildren in England were asked about their smoking, it turned out that the more heavily they smoked, the more likely they were to believe that smoking could help them to keep their figure. In fact, four out of ten smokers believed that 'smoking keeps your weight down' and this was presumably one of the reasons why they continued to smoke. The irony is that teenage smokers actually weigh *more* on average than non-smokers of the same age, a fact which flies in the face of these beliefs.

Even more dismal is the fate of children who take up smoking in the hope of losing weight. One American survey found that overweight boys were much more likely to be thinking about taking up smoking than boys of average weight. Another found that one in five overweight female smokers had taken up smoking specifically for this reason. As they were still overweight, the strategy had obviously failed.

Yet it is my belief that the biggest trap of all is the one which convinces us that we need cigarettes to control our weight. In this book, I hope to convince you that you do not have to reach for a cigarette instead of a sweet. It *is* possible to stop smoking without gaining weight – many successful quitters have done just that. Even if you have spent many years trapped between eating and smoking, it is possible to break free. If you can see the 'smoke to be slim' trap for what it is, then you have taken the first step to a longer, healthier life.

2

THE SLENDER TRAP

With my smoking now ceasing
My food was increasing
And the bills which came in were immense
My vital statistics
Were unrealistic
Things just didn't seem to make sense

The problem of dieting
Was very disquieting
I existed for weeks without dinner
My physique I exerted
And snacks I deserted
But nothing would make me get thinner.

'Smoking' by C. Bailey
Ms London, 21st July 1975.

Smoking is the number one killer in the Western world. One in three smokers are killed by their habit, often 10, 20 or even 30 years before their time. Smoking kills more people than all other drugs, alcohol, suicides and all other known causes of death put together, including AIDS. And for the first time in the history of women's smoking, lung cancer is beginning to overtake breast cancer as their leading cause of cancer death. Stopping smoking is the single most important step that anyone can take to increase their chances of living a longer, healthier life; the drawback is that the advantages of quitting are often seen to be outweighed by the 'disadvantages'. In this case, literally, by the fear of getting fat.

THE FACTS ABOUT SMOKING AND WEIGHT

Reading through a popular women's magazine, my eye was caught by the heading 'Why Ex-Smokers Gain'. 'Many smokers–particularly women', it began, 'are deterred from giving up by the fear of getting fat. And now US researchers have confirmed that ex-smokers *do* tend to gain weight–sometimes gross amounts'. There followed a brief and accurate summary of the facts, and my eyes switched to the end, for the punchline. 'Nevertheless', it concluded, 'many women continue smoking precisely because it keeps their weight down, so research aimed at minimizing weight gain after quitting is urgently needed'. A reasonable conclusion – but I somehow felt that most readers would have found it incredibly disheartening. Nowhere was there any encouragement for smokers who might have been thinking of quitting, much less any sensible advice on how they might avoid weight gain in the meantime. The only real hope was that the research might come up with some sort of a solution – but how long would that take?

I couldn't help but contrast the article with the original report. Drawing its conclusions from the best survey on smoking and weight ever conducted, it was at pains to point out that most people do not gain large amounts of weight when they stop smoking. On the average, it said:

- people who stop smoking gain only 4½-9lb (about 2-4kg), bringing them into line with people who have never smoked.
- half of them gain *even less* than this, and
- only a small number of people who stop smoking experience major weight gain.

The health risks of gaining even a moderate amount of weight would, it stressed, be far outweighed by the health benefits of stopping smoking.

It is a pity to single out a women's magazine for its efforts, as so many women's magazine journalists go out of their way to help their readers to quit, but it does go to show how even the supposed advocates of good health can just as easily end up hammering yet another nail into the coffin. So deeply ingrained is the notion that everyone is locked into a relentless and necessary battle to stay slim, that the real questions go unanswered.

In this chapter I want to show you why it is that so many smokers feel compelled to dice with death in pursuit of a slender figure, and how, in the end, they become trapped into a habit which they neither enjoy nor want to continue.

SLIM IN A FAT WORLD

Many people find slimness an unattainable goal. We are encouraged to be slim, we want to be slim, but we are also encouraged to 'live fat': to eat too much, and do too little.

Let's start with the influence of *variety* on what we eat. For many years, it's been known that people can be encouraged to eat more if they are given more choice, and in the Western world today, there is more choice available than ever before. No longer do we have to walk from butcher to baker to candlestick maker: with every new supermarket which opens, more and more varieties of food become available under one roof, sooner or later to end up under *our* roof, much of it ready to eat in a matter of seconds.

And what a spectacular variety of food it is! We can select, not only from the unprocessed and seasonal foods that our grandparents and great-grandparents once ate, but from mouthwatering displays of exotic and ethnic foods available year round, and from the products of the food revolution – thousands of manufactured foods which, but for advances in technology, would not exist at all. We have become overrun with restaurants, cafés and takeaways and you can be sure that at any time of the day, someone, somewhere will be eating something to make you think of joining them. Variety may be the spice of life, but it is also, as any good chef knows, a source of temptation. And, according at least to one viewpoint, it is one cause of overconsumption in the affluent world today.

Case History

Jane is a 45-year-old mother of three grown up children. Until recently, she was the envy of her friends – one of those lucky people who seemed to be able to eat whatever she wanted, whenever she wanted and not get fat. But when the second of her three children left home, things got out of hand. Instead of acting as family 'chauffeur' and rushing around from A to B coping with the endless round of cleaning, cooking, homework etc., she found herself with time to kill. She started stopping off for coffee and a buttered bun while she was doing the shopping, lingering at the table after supper, trying out new foods from her local supermarket, even experimenting with new recipes – all quite a novelty, until she found the bathroom scales showing an extra 10lb (4½kg).

Faced with this unwelcome addition, Jane decided to take decisive action. It took her about six months to get back to her previous weight, which she did quite easily, except that she became increasingly reliant on her smoking. Always a moderate smoker, she now finds herself lighting up a cigarette to bridge the gap between what she would like to eat, and what she allows herself. Tobacco contains no calories, and feeding her addiction to nicotine now takes priority over satisfying her appetite for food. This is fine, she says, from the viewpoint of staying slim, except that, following a recent attack of bronchitis (during which she lost even more weight) she now wants to quit smoking. But she dare not. Her neighbour (who finds it difficult to stay slim) quit smoking last year and put on quite a lot of weight, and she's often read that stopping smoking makes people fat. She wants to quit, but she cannot imagine how she could lose the weight again . . . without smoking. It's really a question of Catch 22.

A Question of Taste

It is not just the wide variety of foods which make it difficult for us to be slim, but also their nutritional composition. Left to their own devices, infants from the age of weaning will select for themselves an excellent diet which closely matches up to the modern-day view of nutritional need, providing that you are careful to exclude from the choice highly processed foods like sweets, crisps, and biscuits. Include them, and their choice rapidly deviates from the ideal. The simple fact is that sweet-toothed or not, most of us like to eat sweet foods, especially if we are used to eating them, and much the same is true of foods which are high in fat (like chips), particularly if they are also high in sugar (like biscuits).

Food retailers and manufacturers are wise to this, and go to a great deal of trouble to encourage us to eat more and more of the foods we like the 'best'. At the supermarket we find ourselves tempted by strategically placed items on the shelves or check-outs. Watching TV after supper, we are reminded during the commercial break of the chocolate bar we had left in the kitchen for tomorrow, because we thought we had eaten our fill. Driving along the freeway in the USA, the intersections are recognizable not just by the road signs, but by the giant logos of competing hamburger chains. We are talking here not about marketing fresh fruit and vegetables (where is the profit mark-up in a carrot?), but about their designer products – potato crisps and other 'snack' foods, chocolates, sweets, biscuits and breakfast cereals. Taken together, UK advertising expenditure in 1990 on these products amounted to nearly double the amount spent pushing tobacco – almost a staggering £200 million. So tempting are these foods, and so lacking in filling power, that we can easily be 'tricked' into eating more of them than we need to satisfy our nutritional needs, so tipping the balance towards eating too much.

Too Little Exercise; Too Much Worry

The whole situation is compounded by 'modern living'. Thanks to washing machines, dishwashers, central heating, microwaves, food processors, food mixers and any number of other labour-saving devices you care to mention, women have at last been released from a life of constant drudgery – but this has also meant that we tend to take less and less exercise than ever before. Many of us take our cars to the office, spend upwards of 35 hours a week virtually desk-bound, and then drive home and pop a frozen meal into the microwave, or find ourselves at home with little to do, but plenty to eat. We can choose to exercise if we want, but we often have to go out of our way to do it. No longer a necessity of domestic life, physical exertion is fast becoming a luxury which many of us find difficult to fit into our busy lives. The scene is set for easy weight gain, and many of us, even despite considerable efforts to stay slim, find that we have a tendency to get fat. Small wonder then, that next to smoking, obesity is ranked as one of the major public health problems in the Western world. According to recent statistics, some 40 per cent of British men and 30 per cent of British women are overweight, some of them (around 6 million) considerably so. Only the USA and Australasia fare worse.

A Dual Problem

Rachel, a 30-year-old architect and single mother of one, drifts in and out of these obesity statistics from one year to the next. Her problem is a familiar one: stress. It is difficult, she says, to believe that only a couple of years ago, the future had looked so rosy. Her career was going well, her daughter was happy and settled with a local childminder, and personal life was on the up. She joined a gym, lost weight, and recovered much of the self-confidence which had been shattered through a messy divorce. Then came the recession, falling business and childcare problems. As in the past, Rachel finds herself turning to cigarettes and food as an emotional buffer. She is unhappy about her smoking, but regards it as the lesser of the two evils, since weight is the barometer by which she measures her self-esteem. When she feels slim she feels good about herself, when she feels fat, she feels depressed. So she smokes to prevent herself eating.

The irony of this is plain to her. She sees that she eats to comfort herself because she lacks confidence, but she also sees that her lack of confidence is reinforced by her addiction to cigarettes. Smoking has long since been banned in her office, and few of her friends smoke, so she is all too aware that her cigarettes have more control over her than she does over them. Add to this the evidence of the mirror – that smoking is already beginning to spoil her looks – and you can understand why she wants to stop smoking, but also why, as the years go by, she feels less and less sure of her ability to succeed. Last but not least, fifteen years of smoking is beginning to take a toll on her fitness (which also worries her), so putting paid to any plans to lose weight by taking more exercise. It's really a vicious circle.

Slim is Beautiful?

And that's not all. For while Rachel struggles to keep her weight within reasonable limits, she is all too aware that she is not 'slim enough'. Because just as we are encouraged to live fat, so we are pressurized to stay slim. The conflict is not new. Wherever and whenever food has been in abundance, so too has a slender figure been admired and sought after. The difference, however, is that in the 20th century, the notion that 'slim is beautiful' has been given a new and much more powerful impetus through the media.

If you have never stopped to think about the way that the media distorts our vision of the world, then it is worth doing so now. Films, plays, soap operas and advertisements may not be much like everyday life, but after a while the characters we see on our television screens and on the billboards become as 'real' to us as the woman or man next door. But far more actors are slim than the real-life characters they seek to portray; and in 'real life' they will be slimmer still, as they will have 'slimmed for the camera'. Switch on the television, open a magazine, drive past a billboard and you will be met by sylph-like images in various states of undress selling you everything from anti-perspirant to anti-lock brakes, instant coffee to instant sun tan, and, maddeningly, chocolates. We look at ourselves, we look at the models and we find ourselves 'too fat'.

Anorexia Slims

As for the answer, it is right there, in front of your eyes. Cigarettes. As we have seen, cigarettes designed for women (and those most often smoked by them) are low tar, low price (or luxury), longer length and – therefore – slim. At best, this policy reinforces the notion that femininity is equated with elegance and slimness; at worse, it subtly promotes the notion that smoking can make you slim.

Lucinda, a one-time smoker of Silva Thins, is a typical victim of this slender trap. When we met at a counselling session, she told me that she had been battling with her size for years, alternating attempts to quit smoking with attempts to lose weight. To keep her weight under control, she allows herself a meagre 1200 Calories (5020 kilojoules) a day (a dangerously low level), plus a few extra treats at the weekend. Everything she eats has to be rigorously weighed and calorie counted, and she keeps nothing in her bedsit to tempt her to break her diet. When the food runs out, she smokes instead. Not surprisingly, sticking to this plan requires enormous effort. She feels cold and tired and very, very hungry. Smoking is the only way she knows to suppress her hunger, and she relies on it to stop herself from eating, particularly at the end of a meal. Every time she tries to quit smoking, the desire to eat gets the better of her, and finding herself putting on weight, she goes back to smoking for fear that she is at the beginning of a slippery slope to gross obesity.

What makes her problem so sad is that she has never really had a weight problem at all. At worst, she weighed in at 9½ stone (133 pounds/60kg), perfectly healthy for her 5 feet 7 inches (168cm). Yet in search of an elusive 8 stone model goal, she has enslaved herself to a regime of semi-starvation on the one hand and her cigarettes on the other.

The Fashion For Slimness

The other source of our preoccupation with slimness is the fashion industry, which seems at times to be incapable of designing attractive clothes for anyone who is not bordering on the anorexic. Worse still, it acknowledges that the demand for larger sizes is growing, but persists on calling them 'outsize'. As a result, more and more women have to suffer the embarrassment of visiting the 'outsize' department, in the hope of purchasing one of a range of shapeless garments designed 'with our larger customers in mind'. Nor do you have to be particularly fat to find yourself at the mercy of the designer's whim. You may have the legs for this season's micro-skirt, but you cannot guarantee that next season's fashion will suit. Only the superslim can get away with anything; for the rest, shopping can be a frustrating, if not embarrassing, experience.

Clare's Story

Clare, a 25-year-old smoker, knows this to her cost. Even today, she can remember the humiliation of being put on a diet by her mother at the tender age of nine in the hope that she could be squeezed into the latest party dress. As it turned out, the diet was the first of many, and despite countless attempts to lose weight, she now tips the scales at an all-time high.

Eight years ago, however, she thought she'd cracked it. Spurred on by her older sister, she took up smoking, and latched onto it with the same enthusiasm that had earlier sustained her through weeks of crash dieting – only to be unsuccessful again. Sadly, although smoking can help her to get through the day without eating, she says it does not prevent regular binges when she will eat, at one sitting, several bars of chocolate, a packet of biscuits and half a box of cereal, so undermining hours of painful effort. Blaming her lack of 'willpower' for her failure to diet, she resolves to try dieting again, this time more strictly, and so finds herself more deeply trapped in a cycle of overeating, binge eating, smoking, guilt and dieting again.

Smoking and the Metabolic Rate

Despite the evident failure of smoking to control her eating, there is another reason why Clare continues to smoke. Some years ago, she went on a crash diet, and lost a considerable amount of weight in a week, only to put almost all of it back on over two days of Christmas festivities. Drawing the conclusion that she was an 'easy' weight gainer, as she had gained in two days what she had lost in a week, she felt justified in smoking more and more cigarettes, in the belief that smoking dramatically boosts the metabolic rate. In fact, this is wrong on two counts. First, the rapid loss and gain of weight during and after crash dieting is due to changes in the body's water content, not fat, and in common with other obese people, Clare does not have a low metabolic rate. Second, the effect of smoking on the metabolic rate is really quite small and by no means as consistent as she has been led to believe. Although smoking probably increases the metabolic rate in most smokers, recent evidence suggests that it may *decrease* it in some. As Clare rightly deduced, smoking could even be making her fat!

Like Rachel, Clare views smoking to be slim as a vicious cycle. She wants to stop smoking, but above all, she wants to lose weight. She knows that she cannot do both together and she fears that without cigarettes, dieting will become even more difficult. On the other hand, she sees, bitterly, that by continuing with her pack-a-day habit, she is only making a rod for her own back. Taking 10 puffs out of each cigarette means that she is putting something into her mouth 200 times a day, 73,000 times a year. Common sense tells her that if and when she eventually stops smoking she will be tempted to turn to food as a 'cigarette substitute', so compounding the very tendency to overeat which she is trying to control by smoking in the first place.

Like many people, Clare has never even tried to stop smoking, for fear of gaining weight. For years now, she has planned to stop smoking very soon, which is to say as soon as she succeeds in losing weight on yet another crash diet. But most crash diets are far less successful than their proponents would have us believe, and as a result, she ends up trying to tackle one problem, with another even more destructive one.

The Slender Trap

Smoking to be slim is thus a reflection of an attempt to stay slim in a fat world. Like Jane, we may cling to smoking in the mistaken belief that stopping smoking will inevitably make us fat. Like Clare, we may hope that cigarettes will boost our metabolic rate, so that we can eat more, or like Lucinda, we may hope that cigarettes will suppress our hunger so that we can eat less. But smoking does not make people slim, and many smokers, particularly heavy smokers, are also extremely overweight. At best smoking serves to keep the problem at bay. At worst, it is a miserable failure. The irony is that smoking serves only to add to the spiralling loss of self-esteem and worry which is the lot of the chronic dieter, so perpetuating the very problem they seek to control. In consequence, many smokers resign themselves to the belief that they have to smoke to be slim. In the rest of this book I have to convince you that you do not.

3

WHO WANTS A THIN CORPSE ANYWAY?

In this era, when inflation has assumed alarming proportions
and the threat of nuclear war has become a serious danger,
when violent crime is on the increase and unemployment
a persistent social fact, 500 people are asked by the pollsters
what they fear most in the world and 190 answer that their
greatest fear is 'getting fat'.

Kim Chernin
The Obsession

The title of this chapter is attributed to Dr Alton
Ochsner MD, an American physician, who ran a
tireless campaign from the 1940s to establish, in the
face of fierce and vituperative opposition, that
smoking was the leading cause of lung cancer. Among
the many issues he felt strongly about was the use of
cigarettes to sponsor sport, not least the now-infamous
Virginia Slims Tennis Championships. Irritated by the
way that sports sponsorship perpetuated the myth that
it was preferable to be a slim smoker than a non-
smoker, he would ask: 'Who wants a svelte corpse?'

Like Dr Ochsner, many doctors today are sceptical
about smoking to be slim. Some are indeed dismissive,
advising patients that they should 'stop smoking and
worry about the weight afterwards', even saying that
smokers use fear of weight gain as an excuse for

smoking. I can understand why they feel this way, having seen for myself the tragic consequences of smoking. But I know from experience that this advice alienates a smoker who, but for the fear of weight gain, would readily quit. So I am not going to try to persuade you to stop smoking and never mind the consequences for your size. On the other hand, I do want to help you take a balanced view of the issue.

Slim, Fat Or Somewhere In Between?

To start with, how slim are you – and what do you mean by 'slim'? Whenever I talk about this with a group of would-be quitters, it becomes obvious that the word slim means different things to different people. For some, 'slim' means simply 'not fat'. For others, it means more (or less) than this – 'thin' perhaps, or even 'skinny'. And for others, the word 'slim' conjures up more than mere size – thin, elegant and beautiful, or lean, lithe and athletic. About the only thing on which almost everyone agrees is that slim = good.

This doesn't get us very far, so we have to set some limits. As most people who want to stop smoking would like to improve their health, we can usually agree that as a priority we should draw the line between 'slim' and 'fat' on the basis of health or ill-health. We agree not to think of ourselves as 'fat' unless our size puts us at extra risk of illness, and not to think of ourselves as 'slim' unless our size puts us in the low risk category. The next step is to come up with some way of measuring our size, and we usually do this by reference to tables of medically desirable weights.

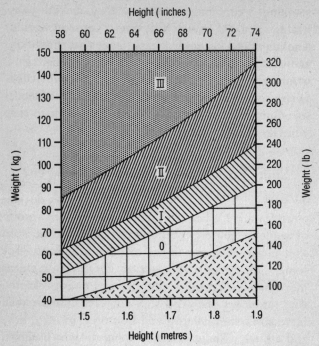

Figure 1 How slim or fat are you? Use your weight and height to find out.
(Source: *Obesity and Related Disorders* (1988) by JS Garrow, with kind permission of Churchill Livingstone Publishers, Edinburgh, UK.)

The chart shown in Figure 1 was developed Professor John Garrow, an international expert on obesity, who divides people into five different categories: from underweight to seriously obese. To work out your own category, first weigh yourself in light clothes and measure your height without shoes. Draw a line across from your weight on the chart, and down from your height. The band in which the two lines meet should help you decide, *on health grounds*, how slim or fat you really are.

Let's start with the dotted area at the bottom of the chart. If you fall into this band, you are underweight, but does it matter? Certainly, the risk of dying young rises considerably in the underweight, but the main reason for this is that most underweight people also smoke. Their low weight may be a sign of an as yet undiagnosed disease like cancer, or it may be the result of years of suffering from a chronic illness like bronchitis or emphysema – and it is this which puts them at risk of an early death. Whether or not it is dangerous to be a bit underweight if you are lucky enough to escape these illnesses is not certain, although there is no doubt that anyone who tries to reduce their weight to lower and still lower levels will eventually become very ill and die.

Anywhere in band O means that you are of normal weight. Providing you stay within this band you can lose or gain weight (as you can see, quite a few pounds in either direction) without affecting your chances of living a long and healthy life. Even if you are not as slim as you would like to be for fashion, the problem for your health is not your weight, but your smoking. In fact, to put things into perspective, take a look at Figure 2, which shows the risk of early death (mortality) in people who smoke and people who don't. The vertical axis of the chart shows their death rate, and the horizontal axis, their body mass index, a good way of measuring obesity. There are two things to notice: smokers are at a much higher risk of death than non-smokers, and the risk of death rises at both ends of the weight spectrum – overweight and underweight. Now consider the risk to a woman smoker who weighs in at 9½ stones (133 pounds/60kg) for her 5 feet 6 inches (168cm). This gives her a Body Mass Index (weight, in kilograms, divided by the square of her height, in metres) of 23.4. According to the graph, her risk of death would be about 1.6 – or 60 per cent higher than average. The Body Mass Index for a non-smoker with the same risk would be 35.7. If she also measured 5 feet 6 inches, then she would weigh in at 14½ stones (203 pounds/93kg), which would put her into Band 2 obesity. *So, it is far more dangerous to smoke than to be overweight.*

This brings us to the other three weight categories: overweight, moderately obese and seriously obese. If you are in Band 1 this means you are overweight and that your health would probably benefit from losing some weight, although there is no degree of urgency about it. Bands 2 and 3 mean that your health is at risk because of your size, mainly from heart disease and diabetes. Dangerous though these conditions are, it is important to appreciate that continuing to smoke for fear of gaining weight doesn't make much sense. Of all the memories which I have of helping people to stop smoking, the one which haunts me the most is of a man who was reluctantly dragged along to a stop smoking group by his workmates. He had wanted to stop smoking for years, but had never done so as he worried about adding to a very serious weight problem which he feared would eventually cause him to have a heart

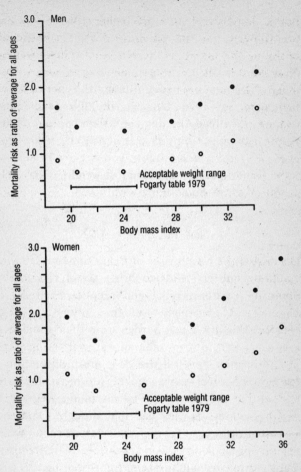

Figure 2 Overweight vs Smoking – and death rates in men and women.

● smoking 20+ cigarettes. ○ never smoked.

Source: 'Obesity: a Report of the Royal College of Physicians', *Journal of the Royal College of Physicians of London*, 1983, with kind permission of the Royal College of Physicians.

attack. Although he knew that smoking was also a risk to his health, he had no idea that it was greatly compounding his risk of the very disease he so wanted to avoid. He needed to stop smoking as well as lose weight, although not necessarily in this order or at the same time. So – if you fall, as he did, into Band 3, and you are not already getting help, then I would advise you to pay your family doctor a visit and talk things over. Let your doctor know you are really serious about wanting to stop smoking/lose weight; it may help if you take this book along with you.

Not Fat After All?

Discussing the health risks of being slim and fat with would-be quitters tends to bring about two totally opposite reactions: relief and scepticism! Relief is common. Underweight smokers often say that realizing this lifts a real burden from their shoulders: they can't wait to stop smoking, eat well and become fit and healthy – even if this does mean putting on a few pounds. Overweight smokers are often surprised to find that they are by no means as overweight, on health grounds, as they had first thought – and this alone helps them to reorder their priorities in favour of stopping smoking as soon as possible. In between are many normal-weight smokers, for whom just talking about their size helps to take the sting out of the issue. From time to time it happens that at this stage an entire stop smoking group (usually between 10 and 25 smokers) will decide that weight is simply not worth worrying about, and there the discussion will end.

Or Not As Slim As You Would Like to Be?

The sceptics come from two camps: those who think that the desirable weights are 'too low' and those who think they are 'too high'. One thing which worries people is the use of weight and height as a way of working out how fat they are. They're right, because it is possible to be heavy without being fat (bodybuilders), or of normal weight while being quite flabby (a couch-potato), but only up to a point. For most of us, there is a very reasonable match between how much we weigh and how fat we are, and in any event, it is sometimes the weight itself which is the cause of problems. People who are overweight are more likely to tire and become short of breath, and they are more prone to trouble with their joints.

Apples and Pears

Talking about this, however, does bring out another issue which I've not yet mentioned: the effect of smoking on your body shape. One of the most important discoveries in the last decade is that some body shapes are a much more important predictor of heart disease and mortality than others. People who are 'apple-shaped' or have most of their fat on their tummy and front are at greater risk than people who are 'pear-shaped', and have most of their fat on their hips, legs and arms. One of the critical measurements is your 'waist-hip ratio'. People who have a large waist measurement compared to their hips are at greater risk than people who have a large hip measurement compared to their waist – and smoking tips the balance in the wrong direction. Even though smokers weigh slightly less on the average than non-smokers, their waist-hip ratio is higher. And the more heavily they smoke, the higher it is. Stopping smoking, on the other hand, improves this picture, and so improves your chances of living a longer and healthier life.

The main objection to the use of medical tables as a basis for defining slimness is, however, that the weights are 'too high'. Overweight smokers may say that the top of the normal weight band is much higher than the goal weight they had set their heart on. Normal-weight smokers who weigh in close to the top of band O say that they feel too fat and want to lose weight, while those who weigh in closer to the bottom of the band feel that they are all right as they are, but would be gross if they let themselves get any bigger. All of this is very understandable, when you consider the pressure on us to be slim, and when you look at the 'goal' weights often set by the writers of commercial slimming books. Many of these are lower than the medical goals, some dangerously so. Furthermore, surveys show that for every woman who is genuinely overweight, there are two who view themselves as such, and want to slim down.

But it is not only the normal-weight and overweight smokers who express reservations about the medically desirable weights. From time to time, I have talked to an obviously underweight smoker who is hell-bent on keeping her figure at all costs, with or without her smoking. I found myself having to point out that this course of action is unlikely to be without its problems. People who stop smoking often seem to experience a resurgence of normal appetite along with a general sense of well-being, and left alone will tend to regain a normal weight. It is one thing to expect to stay underweight if you're a 'natural skinny'–someone who is perhaps very energetic or has a very small appetite, but quite another if you enjoy your food and consequently tend to put on weight quite easily. The less you weigh, the lower your metabolic rate and, therefore, the less food you can afford to eat to stay put. At best you will have to exercise constant restraint over your eating. At worst, you might find that, like Lucinda (page 32) you will end up feeling deprived and hungry.

Worrying About Weight – Why It Can Be Self-Defeating

The real question, though, is whether worrying about your weight really helps you to stay slim. The answer is probably yes – and no. Yes, a certain amount of concern is a good thing for anyone who wants to stay slim in a fat world, but no, too much concern can be a bad thing, at least for some people, some of the time. This may seem illogical, but it is not – as anyone who has frequently tried to lose weight will know. Being preoccupied with weight focuses the mind on eating, or rather not eating, which makes us want to eat all the more!

As a result of this line of thinking, I now ask would-be

quitters who are especially fearful of weight gain to tackle the problem head on. Instead of taking it for granted that worrying about weight is 'natural', we try to think about the reasons behind it. Just getting the worries out in the air can go a long way to resolving them. So, I would like to suggest that you take time to work through your own concerns as part of your preparation for stopping smoking. Remember that the purpose is not to abandon all interest in staying slim (or losing weight if you need to) – there is plenty of advice on how to do this in the rest of the book – but to make it a bit easier on yourself.

HOW SOCIETY SIZES US UP

So why – apart from the obvious influences of the media and the fashion industry – are so many of us so keen to stay slim or lose weight? Here are some of the things which people commonly say, and you may want to add your own personal ones to the list:

- My husband/wife/partner/lover would object
- My friends would disown me if I put on weight
- I'm afraid I'd lose my job
- My clothes won't fit
- I'd be too embarrassed to go on the beach
-
-
-

It is important to see that these concerns stem from the

way our society sizes people up. One of the things I often ask would-be quitters is how much extra weight would worry them – and it often turns out that they are thinking in terms of just 3 or 4 pounds (less than 2kg). When they really stop to think about it, they know that this amount of weight gain would pass unnoticed by anyone except themselves. So what they are really saying is that putting on weight would simply make them feel 'bad' or 'out of control'. Much the same sort of feeling is often expressed by obese people, who see their size as 'sinful' – as if they had a moral duty to grace the world with slender beauty. One look at the history books tells us that this is not true. Throughout the centuries and across cultures, attitudes to fatness have waxed and waned and in some societies, fatness was and still is a sign of wealth, beauty and desirability. Anyone who has looked at Rubens' impressions of the female figure will appreciate that a curvy figure has not always been stigmatized and, on the contrary, has often been greatly admired. The notion that slim is beautiful and fat is ugly is not a moral imperative, but a product of our times.

But does what we look like really have to matter so much? In practice, this question provokes a lot of argument. As we have seen, people clearly feel appearance does matter; and will go to enormous lengths to look good. Among them are models, dancers, actresses and beauty queens, who are rewarded with the adoration of many, but also many ordinary people who are carried along by the flow of the fashionable tide. 'The things we do for beauty' we sigh resignedly, as we embark on yet another diet or exercise plan or struggle into too tight clothes, while we regard with dismay the news that some groups of women have rejected the slim ideal altogether, and have come together to support each other in their right to be fat. Such groups may help their members to feel better about themselves, we say hesitantly, but it takes courage to sport a T-shirt which proclaims that 'big is beautiful' to people who believe otherwise. And anyway, being fat damages your health – which is precisely what we want to avoid by stopping smoking.

What emerges from these debates is that what most people really want is a comfortable middle ground. Yes – we agree that beauty will always be admired, although slim may not always be 'in', but no – we don't want to be judged so harshly by our size, or to spend endless and painful hours trying to attain the unattainable. What about those other qualities – wit, humour, curiosity, passion, intelligence, zest, kindliness and grace? We agree that they matter too. The only difficulty is to find a way of living comfortably in a world which places so great a premium on slenderness. Here then are a few suggestions to help you to become more relaxed about your size.

How Do You Judge Others?

First and foremost, you cannot hope to feel more relaxed about *your* size if you continue to judge other people by *theirs*. And judge them we do – even when we are very young. As toddlers we learn from those lovable characters, Winnie-the-Pooh and Babar the elephant that fat is funny (although even Pooh worries about how tubby he is). Even pre-school children have been found to prefer a slim rag-doll over a fat one – even if they think they are fat themselves. And so it goes on. Research studies have found, variously, that American schoolchildren rate obesity as worse than a series of other physical disabilities, that obese students are less likely to be accepted for college, despite equal level of achievement and application rates; that obese people are less likely to be promoted, that is if they are employed at all; and even that they are less likely to receive an equivalent rate of pay to their leaner executive colleagues.

Even without noticing it we judge people on their size all the time. 'Have you met John's new woman yet?' 'Yes – tall and slim – not his type at all'; 'Met Mrs Jones last week – she looks like the back end of a bus'; 'How was Mauritius?' 'Great – but I ate like an absolute pig and I've put on stones – so I've started this new diet I read about in the Sunday papers and I've lost six pounds already . . .' So start noticing. Notice how often you judge people by their size, and make a conscious effort to stop doing it. How often, when you meet people for the first time, do you find yourself looking wistfully at their slender figure, or thanking your lucky stars that you are not that gross – so much so that you don't even notice anything else about them? What about their other qualities? Do they strike you as

> lively,
> amusing,
> bright,
> witty,

thoughtful,

interesting,

quiet,

happy,

sad,

confident,

and how much does their size really tell you about them? Do slim people really have all the happiness and success? And do you really value your overweight friends any the less because of their size?

Are You Constantly Sizing Yourself Up?

And how do you view yourself? More critically, probably, than you do others. Many people who are conscious of their size jump on and off the bathroom scales several times a week (or several times a day), and endlessly scrutinize their reflection in car doors, mirrors and shop windows. One family I know takes this to extremes and keeps the bathroom scales in the kitchen, so that they can check their weight before deciding on whether or not to have a biscuit! Dieting for them is not so much an occasional necessity as a world view.

If this sounds like you, then now's the time to relinquish the close watch you keep over your size. Unless you are actively trying to lose weight, there is no need to weigh yourself more than once a month, if that – and even if you are actively trying to slim, a fortnightly check is all that is needed. Weighing yourself every day (apart from being very misleading) only concentrates your mind on your size – what you weigh now, what you'd like to weigh, how much weight you want to lose by when, what you had to eat yesterday, what you are going to eat today, when you can next eat . . . and it doesn't help.

LIVING FOR TODAY

Another thing which often hampers would-be quitters who are fearful of weight gain is a reluctance to do today what they could put off until tomorrow. If you spend a lot of time thinking about your size, particularly if you feel you have weight to lose, it is all too tempting to believe that everything will be fine, if only you could reach your goal. 'If I could just get my weight down I could make new friends/attract new lovers/win over Tom, Dick or Harriet/take up skiing/learn a new language/stop smoking . . .' and so forth, setting yourself up for probable disappointment. Being objective can help. What would you like to do or achieve today – and does your size really make it so impossible? Perhaps you don't feel ready to join a mixed swimming team, but do you really have to be slim to learn French/join a choir/go walking with a friend?

IT'S YOUR LIFE

Finally – bear in mind that the attitudes of those closest to you can be destructive. I cannot count the number of times that I have heard a would-be quitter say that their husband/wife/partner/lover would object if they were anything less than superslim, or that their friends would comment on their expanding size. I have met people who have quit smoking to secure their future husband, and I have met people who have tried to diet for the same reason. Yet there is surely nothing more guaranteed to undermine your confidence in yourself or your ability to achieve your goal than the belief that your partner's love and respect for you depends on it. They too have to live in a 'slim world', but you do not need to shoulder their problems as well as your own. Enlist the support of your family and friends if they want to help (page 129) – but make sure the decisions you make about your smoking and your size are yours and yours alone.

4

SMOKELESS FUEL

'Food is an important part of a balanced diet'
Fran Leibowitz
Metropolitan Life, 1978

There are two ways to avoid weight gain when you stop smoking: eat well, and take more exercise. This chapter is about food and eating. There are five key guidelines.

1. **A plan for life**. It is not so much that smoking makes people slim, as that not smoking exposes us to a way of life which can make us fat. So turn the issue on its head. Rather than seeing stopping smoking as an isolated event, look at it as just one part of a gradual change to a way of eating which will make it easier for you to stay slim. Permanently.

2. **One step at a time**. If you are happy with your size now, then all you need to do is stay still. If you want to stop smoking and you also need to lose weight, then take it one step at a time. It's asking too much of yourself to stop smoking and lose weight at the same time, much less go on a strict diet.

3. **Eat well**. The most important thing is to avoid eating to excess – by far the main cause of weight gain in quitters. You may find it helpful to exercise choice over *what* you eat. Smokeless Fuel needs to be low on

fattening power and high on filling power and good taste, so that you can satisfy your hunger and your appetite without eating more calories. If you do find yourself putting on a few pounds over a period of weeks or months as a result of a small drop in your metabolic rate (remember – it may not happen to you) you can reverse the picture by eating just a bit less, or exercising a bit more. You'll probably find this easier once you're over the initial phase of stopping smoking.

4. Eat to live – and enjoy it. There is more to food than fuel. We need to eat, because without food we die, but eating is also one of life's greatest pleasures. Stopping smoking merits celebration, not deprivation. This isn't the time for dull or boring food, and Smokeless Fuel doesn't have to be either.

5. Plan your eating. Finally, there's the question of how we eat, when we eat, and why. Effort invested now in establishing habits which will make it easier for you to stay/get slim will be rewarded many times over in years to come. I've included a special section at the end of this chapter to help you if eating and weight is already a significant problem in your life.

In the rest of this chapter, I want to help you plan ahead so that you can avoid the pitfalls which lead to unwanted weight gain.

A FOOD DIARY

The starting point is to get to grips with your eating habits now, so that you can work out what, if anything, you need to change. One way of doing this is to write down everything you ate yesterday and then think about how you might make a few easy changes, but this isn't really the best approach. Even if you could remember accurately what you ate yesterday (most of us find this amazingly difficult), it probably wouldn't give you a good picture of what you normally eat. You really need to keep a record for at least a week or, better still, a fortnight.

An example of a food diary is shown in Figure 3. You'll need a small notepad that you can carry around with you. Draw up a supply of diaries as shown, and then write down everything you have eaten and drunk *straight away*. Use the left-hand column to record the time and the next to make a note of how much you eat. You don't need to weigh and measure, but you do need to write down some idea of the amount. 'Beef and two veg' won't give you enough information to go on – but '2 slices of beef, three roast potatoes, four tablespoons of peas with fatless gravy' will. This way you can look back and get a really clear idea of how much you eat of different foods.

Use the other three columns to get an idea of *why* you eat. Make a note of anything else you're doing while you're eating, your mood and how hungry you are, on a scale of 0 (not hungry) to 5 (very hungry). Don't worry if you find yourself automatically eating a bit less as a result of keeping a diary – the main thing is to get an idea of what you eat, when you eat and why.

Food Diary: Tuesday

Time	What Eaten	Doing What	Hunger rating	Mood
6.45am	Tea with whole milk, 1 tsp sugar	In bed	3	Waking Up
8.10am	Bowl of wheat cereal, 8 tbsp milk, 2 tsp sugar. Thin slice brown toast, butter and marmalade	Breakfast with children	5	Frazzled
10.25am	Coffee with milk, Chocolate biscuit	Break	1	Relaxing
2.20pm	2 thin slices of bread, about 2oz Cheddar cheese and margarine	Lunch alone	2	Cheery
3.50pm	Can of coke	Waiting in car	1	Bored
6.00pm	Half slice buttered toast	Leftovers	0	Anxious
7.45pm	Glass wine plus handful of peanuts	Cooking	0	Winding down
8.05pm	Spaghetti bolognese: about 3oz pasta, large helping meat sauce. Low fat yogurt	Supper	3	Cheery
10.00pm	Tea with milk and sugar, Biscuit	Watching TV	0	Bored

Figure 3

HOW DO YOU EAT?

The first thing to look at is your eating style. It may be that you eat pretty much the same from day to day – but the chances are that you eat much more on some days than on others – the difference between a weekday and a weekend, for example. This type of eating is typical for most of us, unless we're following a special 'diet', and over time, heavy eating days tend to get balanced out by days when we eat less. But there's a difference between this kind of eating, and eating which is 'all over the place'. Perhaps you eat very little for days on end and then eat a great deal, or never sit down to a meal, but eat endless small snacks while you're doing something else? Perhaps you frequently eat when you're not really hungry, or because you're bored or unhappy? Eating this way can be a real barrier to becoming a slim ex-smoker. It's difficult to keep track of what you're eating and how much – and this puts you at risk of eating more than you need. The risk is that you will end up eating when you would otherwise be smoking, and end up substituting food for cigarettes.

The Chocolate Eclair Syndrome

This is, of course, precisely what quitters' guides recommend. 'If you fancy a cigarette, chew a carrot or an apple instead' runs the advice, which many people find extremely helpful. But it's not without its problems. It's all too easy to end up 'smoking' chocolate eclairs instead. Not only does all this extra eating put you at risk of gaining weight, it also serves as a constant reminder that you would otherwise be smoking. Eating round the clock *can* become a habit, and breaking it is widely regarded as a priority in tackling weight problems.

Meals and Snacks

Prevention is better than cure. So, if you do find yourself wanting a cigarette 'substitute' in the early weeks without smoking, stick with raw vegetables only (see page 70) and make a point of stopping them as soon as you feel able. Apart from this, if you do eat fairly regularly, stick with it, and if you don't, start to break the pattern of irregular eating now. What I suggest is that you aim to eat the conventional three meals a day or, if you find it easier, eat the same *amount* of food, but little and often, say three smaller meals, plus up to three small snacks, taken at fairly regular times in between.

There are a few other valuable tips.

- When you are eating, make sure you concentrate on eating, rather than on the TV or whatever else you happen to be doing at the time.
- Make a point of noticing what you're eating – the colour, aroma, texture and taste, and slowly savour each mouthful, so that the feeling of satisfaction has time to catch up with you.
- If you are in the habit of finishing up every last mouthful on your plate even when you know

you've had enough, try leaving something on your plate.

- If you're responsible for cooking meals, make just enough for one helping, unless you have definite plans to use the leftovers for another meal.
- When you have finished eating, get up from the table and start doing something else. This way you're less likely to notice the absence of a cigarette, and less likely to carry on eating for eating's sake.

Guidelines, Not Rules

Having said this, it's important not to be too rigid in your thinking. These are a set of general guidelines, not rules to be followed at all costs and then recklessly broken. There are bound to be one-off occasions when you *want* to eat outside of your usual times – say at an unexpected social event – and there is no reason to feel guilty if you do eat something when you didn't plan to. Don't be surprised if you sometimes find yourself eating almost without realizing it, or using food as a cigarette substitute. You would be unusual if you didn't. The best aim is to eat regularly, most of the time – not rigidly, all of the time.

WHAT DO YOU EAT?

Now think about what you eat, and what you are going to eat when you quit smoking. Remember that the objective is not to eat less, but to find a way of eating more satisfying food without eating more calories. All you really need to know can be summarized by the note I used to have pinned up over my desk which read:

- Fat Fattens
- Starch Satisfies
- Sugar Merely Sweetens.

Fat Fattens

If you never remember anything else, remember this. Our food is made up of three main nutrients: fat, carbohydrate (starches and sugar) and protein and of these, fat is the most fattening of all. Weight for weight, pure fat contains around twice as many calories as pure carbohydrate or pure protein – and it doesn't matter whether the fat is saturated, monounsaturated or polyunsaturated (although for the sake of your heart, you may want to limit your intake of saturates in particular). This alone means that fat is more fattening. But this isn't the only problem. Fatty foods like margarine or butter tend to be almost pure fat, whereas starchy foods like bread and potato contain a lot of water. So mouthful for mouthful, fatty foods contain far more calories than starchy foods, which is what nutritionists mean when they say that fatty foods are 'calorie dense'. The upshot is that the butter you put in your jacket potato could easily contain as many calories as the potato itself.

The positive side of this is that small changes count. You probably wouldn't want to eat your potato without butter – but could you use half the amount, or use a low-fat spread instead? Using ½oz of butter instead of an ounce (1 oz = 28 grams) will save you around 100 Calories (420 kilojoules); switching from butter to the same amount of low-fat spread will achieve roughly the same result. If you could make just three small changes like this every day, then you would have 300 Calories (1250 kilojoules) in hand, to use on something more filling.

Starch Is Satisfying

This is where starch comes in. Fat has been getting a lot of criticism of late, but this has been matched by a real boost for starchy foods like bread, potatoes, and pasta. From our point of view, their most important property is their filling power. All starchy foods are filling, and some people find the high-fibre foods especially so – the added advantage being that fibre supplies almost no calories. Some more sums. A steaming bowl of minestrone soup, packed with fresh vegetables and pasta, plus a thick slice of wholemeal bread, might set you back say, 300 Calories – depending on the recipe, how thickly you slice the bread and so forth. So would half a small pork pie. Which has the greater filling power? Opt for the pork pie and it will be gone in a mouthful, leaving you wondering what to eat next. Opt for the soup and bread and you have a meal which will be a good deal more filling and will certainly take longer to eat. If stopping smoking makes you feel hungry, then filling up on high-starch, low-fat foods like bread, fruit and vegetables, makes sense.

Sugar Merely Sweetens

This brings me to sugar – by which I mean white sugar, brown sugar, invert sugar, cane, muscovado and demerara sugars, glucose, fructose, dextrose, lactose and maltose, syrup *and honey*. Sugar sweetens. No more; no less. It contains no other nutrients – no protein, no fibre, no vitamins or minerals to speak of, just calories. This alone makes it a prime target for cutting down on – but it's not the only problem. How often do you eat pure sugar? You may put it in tea or coffee or on your cereal, but more often than not, sugar comes in biscuits, cakes, chocolate etc. – which also contain fat – and also in a surprising number of processed savoury foods, like sauces and cheese spread. This means that sweet foods are also often high in fat. It's not that you should never again eat high-sugar, high-fat foods – but it makes a lot of sense to eat less of them.

FOOD, GLORIOUS FOOD

To sum up, Smokeless Fuel means less fat and less sugar, and more starchy foods like bread and pasta, and more fruit and vegetables. But it doesn't mean brown rice and lentils. Smokeless Fuel can be warming and comforting, hot and spicy, or fresh, simple and homely. For me (and I write as a devotee of chocolate fudge cake), Smokeless Fuel conjures up two very different pictures. One is of a cold winter's night, a glowing fire, a warming casserole and a piping hot jacket potato, followed by a steaming baked apple spilling over with hot dried fruit. The other is of a warm summer's evening on an Italian beach; a table laid with pasta, freshly grilled fish, a simple salad of tomatoes and fresh herbs dressed with a little olive oil, and warm apricots and peaches to follow. Even if this kind of eating doesn't appeal to you, take heart: this is just my personal choice. We all have our food likes and dislikes, and by and large we tend to like what we are used to. On the other hand, people often say that stopping smoking improves their sense of taste, and our likes and dislikes are not fixed for life. In fact, most changes are easy, as long as you don't make up your mind that they're going to be difficult. So – resolve to make a few gradual changes in your eating, and make them part of your plan to become slim without smoking. You don't have to make all of them, or any of them, all of the time. At the end of the suggestions you'll find some examples of how two would-be quitters adjusted their daily eating patterns.

Ways to Cut Your Fat Intake

- Switch from whole milk to semi-skimmed or skimmed. If you can't face semi-skimmed, start with unhomogenized whole milk (silver top) and pour away the cream.
- Switch from butter or margarine to a low-fat spread, and spread it thinly.
- Switch from full-fat cheese like cheddar to medium-fat varieties like half-fat cheddar or Brie or Edam, or low-fat cottage and curd

cheeses. Cheese goes further in sandwiches or potatoes if you grate it. If you're after a cheesy flavour (in a sauce or topping), use the strongest cheese you can find, but in smaller quantities, and season generously with mustard and pepper.

- Choose poultry and game rather than red meats. Roast, grill or bake without fat, and remove the skin.
- Look for the new leaner cuts of beef, lamb and pork, and trim off as much visible fat as possible. Grill or roast slowly without extra fat.
- Choose fish and shellfish more often. Grill, bake or poach, rather than batter and fry.
- Use as little fat and oil as possible in cooking, and serve vegetables and potatoes without butter or rich sauces. Grill, boil, bake in foil, microwave and steam without added fat rather than deep-frying, frying and roasting.
- Casserole or stew cheaper cuts of meat without frying first, and remove any fat which comes to the surface. Try replacing part of the meat with extra vegetables or tomatoes.
- Thicken sauces with cornflour rather than a flour and fat 'roux'.
- Substitute low-fat yogurt for mayonnaise, cream or strained (Greek style) yogurt.
- Save fatty biscuits, cakes, puddings, pies, processed meats, sweets and nuts for special eating – rather than every day.

Ways to Eat More Starch

- Eat more breakfast cereals – wholewheat, sugar-free varieties.
- Eat more potatoes – jacket baked, boiled in their skins or roasted without fat. To do this, parboil and roast separately on a heatproof glass dish for 1 hour at 180°C. You can also make chips (French fries) this way.
- Eat more pasta – it comes in all shapes, sizes and colours and in wholemeal varieties too – tomato-based sauces are ideal.
- Eat more bread – especially wholemeal, but also multigrain, rye and corn bread and the many varieties of rolls, bagels and continental breads too. Cut thicker slices and use less fatty fillings and spreads.
- Eat more rice – brown and white, and try out other grains, like couscous, bulgur wheat, and barley. Brown rice has an undeservedly bad reputation. Experiment with an easy-cook variety.
- Eat more vegetables (fresh and frozen), salads and beans and pulses (including baked beans and other tinned varieties) – steam, boil, or microwave without fat.
- Think backwards. Rather than plan on the meat and then add potatoes as an afterthought, start with the starchy item – say rice or pasta and then add a little meat, fish or cheese. If you would normally eat lamb chops and two veg, try a vegetable and lamb risotto instead.

- Eat more fruit – fresh raw fruit, steamed fruit and tinned fruit in natural juice – local produce and exotic varieties too.

Ways to Eat Less Sugar

- Switch from fizzy drinks and squashes containing sugar to low and no sugar varieties.
- Switch to unsweetened breakfast cereals – some contain up to 50 per cent sugar.
- Reduce and then cut out sugar in tea, coffee and on breakfast cereals.

Case History

Allison is an ex-twenty-a-day smoker who really enjoys her food. She's not too keen on salads and was altogether very wary of the idea of 'healthy' eating. Here's how she adjusted one day's usual eating for greater satisfaction value. The italics mark places where she cut back on fat or sugar or switched to low-fat, low-sugar or high-fibre alternatives. Bold type marks all the extra food she was able to eat as a result. Both menus contain roughly the same number of calories.

Usual eating	Smokeless Fuel
Breakfast	
Coffee with *whole milk*	Coffee with *semi-skimmed milk*
Cereal with *whole milk*	Cereal with *semi-skimmed milk*
Slice toast with *margarine*	Slice toast with *low-fat spread*
	Extra slice toast, low-fat spread
Snack	
Coffee with *whole milk*	Coffee with *semi-skimmed milk*
Banana	Banana
Lunch	
2 slices *brown bread and butter*	2 slices *wholemeal bread, low-fat spread*
2oz/55g *Cheddar cheese*	2oz/55g *half-fat Cheddar*
	Extra slice wholemeal bread, low-fat spread
	Fruit yogurt
1 can *sweetened fizzy drink*	1 can *sugar-free fizzy drink*
Snack	
Tea with *whole milk and sugar*	Tea with semi-skimmed milk
Chocolate biscuit	Chocolate biscuit
1 glass of wine	1 glass of wine
Supper	
3oz/85g pasta (dry weight)	3oz/85g pasta
	Extra 1oz/30g pasta
Large helping meat sauce	Large helping tomato and meat sauce
Stewed apple and *thick cream*	
	Stewed apple and *diet yogurt*
Coffee with *whole milk*	Coffee with *semi-skimmed milk*
Late night snack	
Tea with *whole milk and sugar*	Tea with *semi-skimmed milk*
	Currant bun, low-fat spread

Case History

Patricia saw herself as a 'classic smoker'. Black coffee and cigarettes for breakfast, a snack lunch and just one meal in the evening. She said she often felt hungry between meals, and didn't see how she was going to be able to stop smoking without feeling permanently starved. Making changes was easier than she expected – the main problem was finding room for all the extra food. Both menus contain roughly the same number of calories.

Smoke-Free Snacks

It's not easy to find snacks which are low in fat and high in starch. Here are ten suggestions – listed starting with the lowest in calories. The bigger snacks are really small meals – ideal if you plan on eating 'little and often'.

- Assorted vegetable 'crudités' – carrot, celery, tomato, cucumber, peppers etc.
- One apple, orange, pear, or peach
- One very low-fat fruit or 'diet' yogurt
- One semi-sweet biscuit
- One banana
- One small bag (about 1oz/28g) of low-fat crisps
- One slice bread (about 1oz/28g) plus low-fat spread
- One slice bread, topped with two tbsp baked beans, no butter or fat
- One currant bun, no butter or fat
- Sandwich made with two small slices of bread and filled with tuna (drained of brine) and cucumber, cottage cheese and tomato, a small banana, or chicken & chutney

Usual eating	Smokeless Fuel
Breakfast	
Black coffee	Black coffee
Black coffee	Black coffee
	Cereal & semi-skimmed milk
	Slice toast, low-fat spread
	Grilled mushrooms
Snack	
Black coffee	Black coffee
Lunch	
2 slices *toast and butter*	2 slices toast, *no butter*
Baked beans	Baked beans
Can *sweetened fizzy drink*	Can *sugar-free fizzy drink*
Snack	
Black coffee	Black coffee
Apple	Apple
	Digestive biscuit
Supper	
Fried chicken (battered), chips, peas	*Roast chicken, no skin*
	Dry roast potatoes, peas
	Instant fat-free gravy
2 rum and *sweetened cola*	2 rum and *diet cola*
Small packet *peanuts*	Small packet *low-fat crisps*
Late night snack	
Black coffee	Black coffee
	Sandwich: 2 slices wholemeal bread, tuna, tomatoes

IF EATING IS A PROBLEM . . .

I end this chapter with a special section for anyone who is struggling to deal with a smoking problem *and* an eating problem. If you have spent many years battling to

71

stay slim or lose weight, perhaps alternating periods of strict dieting with overeating or bingeing, then it may seem to you now that the situation is hopeless. You cannot control your eating when you are smoking – so how can you possibly hope to control it when you are not? I know because I've been there, and while I don't want to pretend for a moment that I have 'the key', I do know that it can be tackled. People *can* successfully lose weight and stop smoking, and there is every reason to give it a go.

One Step At a Time

What I suggest is that you tackle the problem in a series of small manageable steps, rather than letting yourself feel overwhelmed by it. The first step is to work towards a more relaxed style of eating, so that you can stay at a stable weight without dieting. This alone should help you to feel more relaxed about your size, but if you are very overweight, or if your size makes you feel very unhappy, you should next bring your weight down to a more comfortable level. When you have done this, stop smoking, consolidate your new eating habits, and then, if you want to, slim down further.

Of course, this isn't the only approach, but I think it's a good one. You will find it easier to stop smoking without gaining weight if you first get on top of your eating, but it's equally important not to delay stopping smoking for too long. Quite apart from the health risks, smoking, which involves putting something into your mouth many times a day, is not a very good way of dealing with an eating problem. Sooner or later, you want to stop smoking, and the sooner you do it the better. You will be rewarded with an enormous boost to your confidence, and this in turn will help you to see your project through.

You Are Not Alone

First and foremost, realize that you are not alone. Although there are people who have lost weight successfully and maintained their weight for many years, there are many who have tried to lose weight and have failed. The fact that you find it difficult to lose weight does not make you a failure – on the contrary, many people who find it difficult are enormously successful in other areas of their life. Dieting is commonplace, supporting a multi-million pound industry, but most of us are not getting any slimmer.

Dieting Needs to be Handled with Care

One reason probably lies in the nature of dieting itself. We gain weight slowly, but we want to lose it quickly. To do so means exercising restraint over how much we eat, and the more quickly we want to lose it, the more restraint we have to exercise. Up to a point, restraint is a good thing. It's helpful to have an idea of which foods contain the most calories and which the least, and to be able to say 'no' when you've had enough. But too much restraint can be counterproductive. We try to eat less, and instead end up eating more. This makes us feel guilty so we try to cut back even further, which

73

we find even more difficult, and so on. Instead of becoming less and less interested in food and eating (which would help us to get/stay slim), we instead become preoccupied by it. It is against this background that some of us turn to smoking to help us maintain a fragile control over our size, and so become trapped ever more deeply into the cycle of dieting, overeating, guilt, smoking, guilt, dieting and overeating again.

How to Become More Relaxed About Eating

When you have thought this through, I hope it will become obvious that your first step must be to break the cycle. You have to give up active attempts to lose weight, and learn to adopt a more regular eating pattern. The advice is the same as given on pages 60–71, but be prepared to make progress very gradually.

First, work towards a more regular eating pattern. This has a lot of advantages for anyone who wants to become slim without smoking:

- It's convenient – you'll be eating when most other people eat, and you won't have to feel deprived.
- It will help you to become less preoccupied with food. You won't have to worry about whether and when you can next eat – but the next meal will never be too far away.
- You won't ever become excessively hungry,

but you will be in tune with the usual cycle of hunger, fullness, slowly returning hunger, and so on. Make a point of noticing how much more you enjoy your food if you do wait until you feel hungry. And start to cultivate a positive dislike of feeling too full.

- By limiting your eating to only a few times a day, you will automatically avoid eating for emotional reasons – like boredom, worry or anger. This will encourage you to look for other more constructive ways of dealing with them: see Chapter 7.

Establishing a regular meal pattern will take time, especially if you are not used to eating this way. So to begin with, don't worry so much about *what* you are eating as *when*. Decide when you would like to eat your meals and snacks, and then work towards not eating in between, starting with the time you would find easiest. So – suppose, for example, that you decide to aim for breakfast, lunch and supper, plus a late night snack, because you know that evening is your most difficult time. Your first objective might be to not eat between breakfast and lunch, and you should try to master this first before moving on to the afternoon. Once you've got this under your belt as well, you could tackle the evening – so that you eventually reach the point when you're eating fairly regularly, most of the time. It's important not to be too hard on yourself if you do lapse and find yourself eating when you didn't intend to. Ask yourself *why* it happened (were you perhaps bored – in which case what could you have done instead?), and then put it behind you.

While you are working on *when* you eat, start thinking about *what* you eat. Many people who worry about their weight go out of their way never to buy this or that, instead restricting themselves to a monotonous 'diet' of allowed foods. For weeks at a time they resolve never again to eat chocolate, cookies, cup cakes or cheese, only to succumb in the end to temptation when all are consumed hastily, amid feelings of guilt and self-loathing. So, if you too have a list of banned foods, start now to reintroduce them gradually. Once you are eating less frequently, you can afford to eat more at each meal, and while I am not suggesting that you go mad and eat with abandon, you should be able to eat foods you enjoy. Don't worry too much if at first you find it difficult to limit your eating of previously 'banned' foods – after all, absence makes the heart grow fonder. A time will come when these foods no longer seem so tantalizing and irresistible, and you will gradually be able to work towards eating more carefully.

Is There a Place for Smoke-Free Dieting?

In recent years, there has been a spate of anti-diet books, which take much of what we have been talking about to its logical conclusion. Dieting can make people preoccupied with food and weight, so don't diet. In principle, this is very sound advice for anyone who has no real need to diet, but it isn't so helpful if you *do* have a medical need to slim. It's a pity to take the trouble to stop smoking without also reducing your weight to healthy levels, and in this situation, dieting can help.

The important thing is to choose a way of losing weight which will not undermine your ability to stay slim long term. For this, I suggest the following guidelines.

1. Don't try to lose too much weight too quickly. A weight loss of between 1 and 2lb (about ½-1kg) a week is the maximum you should aim for (although you may lose more in the early stages). This means that crash dieting it out.

2. Don't carry on dieting if you are finding it really difficult. Go back to normal eating for a week or so, until you feel ready to continue. It will take longer, but the results are more likely to be permanent.

3. In the first instance, try adapting your plan for Smoke-Free Eating for weight loss. All you need to do is cut down further on your intake of fatty foods *without* replacing them by extra starch. According to recent research, people who do this find it very difficult to make up the lost calories, because of the sheer bulk of the diet. So, they lose weight.

4. If you prefer to follow a more definite plan, choose one of the many diet guides available in bookshops and libraries. Check for sound principles. All diets which work (i.e. you lose fat, not water) work because they reduce your calorie input from food below your calorie output. So the diet should be low in calories,

but not too low – no less than 1000 Calories (4200 kilojoules) a day for women and 1500 Calories (6250 kilojoules) for men. Look for one which is low in fat and sugar, and includes a wide variety of foods.

5. If you enjoy tackling problems with other people, set up a self-help group with like-minded friends, or join a slimming group, but check it out first. Make sure it's run by a reputable organization, and that they don't hand out diuretics or other drugs, without first referring you to your own doctor. The diets should be based on sound principles (see above) and the help should be supportive, not critical. You shouldn't be made to feel guilty if you are finding it difficult to lose weight or if you want to slow down for a bit. There should be help with adjusting to your new slimmer size, and advice on how to stay slim.

6. Bear in mind that when you have lost weight you will need less food. This is not because dieting abnormally reduces your metabolic rate (it doesn't, unless you reduce your calorie intake to well below the levels I've suggested), but because bigger bodies burn up more calories. So – gradually increase your food intake until you find a level at which you can stay comfortably slim without smoking.

SOME QUESTIONS AND ANSWERS

Q A friend of mine quit last year and says she put on seven pounds in a month, even though she doesn't remember eating more than usual. Could this be because of a fall in her metabolic rate?

A No, it couldn't. Although metabolic rate does fall in some quitters, the drop is really quite small and couldn't possibly account for anything like this amount of weight gain in such a short period. Stopping smoking tends to throw people off their normal routine, so it's very easy to overeat without realizing, particularly between meals. The results can be very disheartening, so it's worth keeping a watchful eye over what you're eating and when, right from day 1.

Q Will I feel very hungry when I quit smoking?

A Not everyone feels extra hungry when they first quit, and only a few feel very hungry. Eating a high-starch, low-fat diet with plenty of fruit and vegetables is the best way of coping.

Q Is it a good idea to cut down on coffee when you quit smoking? I've heard that it helps.

A Many stop smoking guides recommend this. One reason has to do with association: many people drink coffee and smoke at the same time, so coffee can remind them of smoking. The other reason has to do with the fact that stopping smoking can lead to a doubling of caffeine levels in the bloodstream which could cause some of the 'jittery' feeling which are ascribed to tobacco 'withdrawal'. But cutting down on coffee has not been shown to consistently influence people's success in stopping smoking. One disadvantage is the loss of caffeine's possible stimulatory effects on the metabolic rate. The effect is quite small, but losing it could, over a long period of time, result in a small amount of weight gain. On balance then, it's probably best to carry on as usual when you first quit, unless you find that drinking coffee really makes you want to smoke. In the longer term, you may want to cut down on coffee for the sake of your heart. The evidence is that unfiltered, strong, boiled coffee can increase your risk of an attack. But most experts agree that a few mugs of instant or filter coffee won't cause problems.

Q What about alcohol?

A Like sugar, alcohol supplies calories, but no other nutrients – so it doesn't make much sense to drink a lot if you want to stay slim or lose weight. The other thing to be aware of is that it can increase the desire to smoke, and decrease your potency to resist it. Either way, it's sensible to keep your drinking within safe limits. Experiment with low-alcohol drinks (they're improving all the time), or try mixing normal beer with a low-alcohol beer (these also tend to be lower in calories). If you want to enjoy a celebratory drink when you quit but find that drinking makes you want to smoke, avoid the pub or parties, and share a drink with a non-smoking friend in the privacy of your own home.

Q If I cut back on fatty foods, or switch to low-fat varieties, how much extra starch can I afford to eat without increasing my total calorie intake – surely the system can be 'sabotaged'?

A Yes it can, although you may find that you simply can't eat enough bulky foods to replace the lost calories from fat. The only way to be sure is to count calories – but although this approach suits some people, it can easily become a habit which takes the fun out of eating. What's much more important is to eat a varied diet and to have a general feel of which foods are fattening and which foods are not. If you do find yourself gaining weight, just cut back a bit further on fat, or if you feel you have reached your limit, ease up on the extra starch. If you find yourself losing weight, do the reverse.

Q How often can I afford to splash out on high-fat high-sugar foods like puddings and sweets?

A This depends on what you eat the rest of the time. If you tend to eat quite sparingly during the week when you're busy, you can afford to let up more at the weekends than you can if you tend to eat similar amounts from one day to the next. If you eat out only rarely, you can afford to relax much more than if you eat out every day.

Q Isn't it very expensive to eat this way?

A This is a question of swings and roundabouts. Lean meat is usually more expensive than fatter cuts and meat products like sausages, pies and processed meats, and fresh fruits and vegetables can be costly too, especially if you choose out-of-season produce. On the other hand bread, potatoes, rice, pasta and other grains are cheap – and there are savings to be made on high-fat high-sugar foods. When you quit you may be able to spare some cash for a few luxury items – what about treating yourself to some out-of-season strawberries?

Q I already keep a very careful eye on what I eat – so how can I cut back further?

A One would-be quitter who found herself in this position succeeded in quitting smoking with very little difficulty. She made a point of taking extra exercise, and even though she did eat a bit more than usual when she first quit, her generally careful approach to eating helped to minimize the damage – and within a few months she was slimmer than she had been to start with.

Q I'm not sure that I could make the switch to low-fat milk/wholemeal bread.

A It's all a matter of personal preference, but you may not find it as difficult as you think, especially if you make changes gradually. Don't be put off by past experience – today's low-fat milks and diet drinks taste quite different from the old style dried and saccharin-redolent varieties. Sales of low-fat milk, low-fat spreads and wholemeal breads are on the increase – a lot of people like them.

Q What about the rest of the family?

A Smokeless Fuel doesn't have to be different from what everyone else is eating, and you won't need to cook special meals for yourself. Eating habits are formed very early and tend to stick, so you will be doing your children a favour if you keep sweets, cakes and biscuits for special occasions while they are still young. Children under two need full-fat milk. Once they are eating a wide variety of other foods they can be switched to semi-skimmed.

Q Is it a good idea to choose 'low fat' varieties of manufactured foods?

A Yes – but labels can be misleading, and the basis for making a claim like 'low fat' or 'low sugar' varies from country to country. The only way to be absolutely sure is to read the nutrition information food label – and compare it with the normal product.

A good cut-off point for a low-fat product is 5g or less of fat, per serving. Watch out for descriptions like 'all natural' or 'full of healthy goodness' – which are virtually meaningless! For 'full of energy' read 'full of calories'.

Q Do I need to take extra vitamins and minerals?

A Smokers generally have lower blood levels of some vitamins than non-smokers, and some stop smoking guides recommend taking supplements to 'make good the difference'. A multi-vitamin pill a day will certainly do you no harm, but there's no evidence that it will do you much good either once you quit, providing that you're eating a varied diet including plenty of fruit and vegetables.

Q Are there any special foods I can eat which will make stopping smoking easier?

A One popular theory is that eating certain foods can speed up or decrease the rate at which nicotine (the addictive chemical in tobacco) leaves the body. Actually, almost all the nicotine in your body leaves it within 24-48 hours whatever you eat, so the theory doesn't have much going for it in practice.

PLANNING AHEAD

Use this section of the book to write down any changes which you plan to make when you quit smoking. Add to the list any changes that you're prepared to try out –

and be sure to give yourself a few weeks to get used to them.

_____

_____

_____

_____

_____

_____

_____

_____

_____

5

BURNING IT UP

Afoot and light-hearted I take to the open road
Healthy, free, the world before me,
The long brown path before me leading wherever I
    choose.

Henceforth I ask not good fortune, I myself am good
    fortune,
Henceforth I whimper no more, postpone no more, need
    nothing,
Done with indoor complaints, libraries, querulous
    criticisms,
Strong and content I travel the open road.

Leaves of Grass
Walt Whitman.

A PERSONAL EXPERIENCE

I was never a great one for exercise. I did my bit at school, and then gave up. I hadn't enjoyed freezing to death on the hockey pitch, and I certainly didn't intend carrying on with it if I didn't have to. From time to time I went to watch other people playing sport, but that was as far as it got.

Then came my decision to quit smoking. I had heard that stopping smoking could cause my metabolic rate to drop (which I now know may not be true of all people) and I didn't want to put on weight as a result. Either I was going to have to eat less, or I was going to have to get on the move. I decided on swimming. I'd done it at school and quite enjoyed it, and I could walk to the swimming pool on my way to work. It was a simple question of arithmetic: if I was going to burn up fewer calories by stopping smoking, then I would have to burn up more calories through exercise.

Needless to say, I didn't embark on the plan with much enthusiasm. On the first day I spent ages in the changing room toying with the idea of taking my clothes off, and then sat on the side of the pool for a long time, wondering how cold the water was. When I did finally take the plunge I managed only a few lengths and even then, they were quite an effort. I was incredibly unfit – which, considering the years of smoking, was only to be expected.

As the days and weeks passed, my attitude began to change. I don't want to sound evangelical, but it was a lot easier than I'd expected. Instead of dragging myself down to the pool once or twice a week, I decided to go four or five times, and when I got to the point where I missed it if I didn't go, I thought I'd cracked it. I now looked forward to diving into the pool; to the surge of cool, refreshing water around me, and to the feeling of exhilaration and tingling warmth when I got out. I still found the dressing and undressing a hassle, but the freedom of being able to move in the water unhindered by layers of clothes and other baggage made up for it.

Swimming served as a marker of my new-found fitness. Every time I went I clocked up a few more lengths until I was swimming for half an hour or more;

I no longer felt exhausted and lethargic, I positively glowed with health and well-being. Taking exercise was the opposite of a vicious cycle. After a swim I felt more energetic, not less, so I walked the rest of the way to work instead of taking the bus, and then, on my way home, rushed round the supermarket instead of dawdling. I no longer needed so much sleep, but when I did sleep, I slept better. Of course it was impossible to say how much of this was due to stopping smoking and how much to starting exercise, but I'm not sure how much I would have been able to achieve one without the other.

Later, when I began working for QUIT, the charity which helps smokers to stop, I discovered that exercise was one of the most frequently recommended skills for would-be quitters. One quitter told me how important exercise had been for improving her morale:

> 'After spending so many years neglecting my body – smoking and the rest, I just wanted to do everything I could to reverse the damage. Looking after myself made me feel so much better, so much younger and more in control of things. It's given me a real sense of achievement.'

You would think from this that she was in her fifties. Actually, she was only 25, and for the first time in her adult life, understanding what it felt like to be fit. So impressed had she been that she persuaded her friend to try exercising too, but this time with different results.

> 'When I first quit smoking, I felt very uptight without a cigarette to get me through the day. I got into the habit

where if I felt like taking it out on the kids, I went and took it out on the pavement – just running round the block instead. I don't feel so tense anymore, but I've decided to keep the exercise up anyway'.

Her thoughts were echoed by a middle-aged accountant, who had feared that without smoking, he wouldn't be able to concentrate. Instead he found that his concentration was better than ever before:

'I was surprised at how much more alert I felt after I'd done some exercise' he told me. 'Even if I started out feeling really drowsy and not fit for anything, I ended up feeling quite on top of things. Exercise gave me much more of a lift than eating a bar of chocolate, or smoking a cigarette'

And so it went on. For many of the quitters I've met, exercise has been a real lifesaver – a way of relaxing and winding down, a way of enjoying themselves or beating mild depression, a way of making new friends, a way of getting slim and staying slim, and quite simply a way of feeling great.

Does This Mean Climbing Mount Everest?

It sounds impressive, but how much do you have to do to make it worthwhile? Perhaps you've seen one of those depressing calculations which compares the calorie content of a bar of chocolate with the calorie cost of exercise, and comes up with the pronouncement that you would have to 'walk up Mount Everest to walk off a Mars Bar'. This is a wild exaggeration – but the principle is correct. Suppose you're a woman of average weight who wants to lose weight at the rate of around a pound a week. To achieve this you would have to burn up an extra 500 calories a day, equivalent to around two and a half hours' brisk walking – on top of what you normally do. So – unless you have very little else to do, exercise isn't going to be a very practical way of actually losing weight, unless you're prepared to lose it very slowly. It needs to be combined with dietary change as well.

Staying Slim in a 'Fat' World

But exercise *is* a good way of avoiding weight gain when you stop smoking. It can help to counteract the small drop in metabolic rate which some people experience when they quit smoking. And if your metabolic rate doesn't drop, you might actually *lose* a few pounds into the bargain! You'll find that exercise is a good way of balancing out the eating excesses of a 'fat' world. And it's an important factor in helping people who have lost weight to keep it off.

There's also the question of what type of exercise is best. Some types build stamina and endurance, some help to make you more supple and some give you strength. Broadly speaking, it's the ones which help to build up your endurance (often called 'aerobic' exercise) which are best suited to helping you stay slim. And there's an added bonus. Done regularly, aerobic exercise may protect against heart disease – so adding to the health benefits you're already going to achieve by stopping smoking.

As for the exact choice of exercise, it is virtually unlimited from

> aerobics classes to
> badminton,
> basketball,
> dancing,
> football,
> golf,
> hiking,
> hill climbing,
> judo,
> karate,
> keep-fit,
> rock climbing,
> rowing,
> running,
> sailing,
> skiing,
> skipping,
> swimming,
> tennis,
> trampolining,
> volleyball,
> water polo,
> water skiing and
> windsurfing

– and my list is not exhaustive. Some of these will burn up more calories than others, depending on how heavy you are, how energetically you do them, how often you do them, and for how long – but all of them can help you to stay slim without smoking. And if sport doesn't appeal, there are plenty of ways of taking exercise without ever having to set foot on a hockey pitch.

Here are my 'top five'. I suggest that you aim to exercise three or four times a week, more if it appeals. If you don't want to do the same type of exercise each time, you could tot up smaller amounts of different types to achieve the same overall effect.

Walking

Walking can be done almost anywhere, anytime – for pleasure, relaxation – or simply for getting from A to B. Whether you decide to spend a quiet afternoon walking across a park, or a weekend hill climbing, or simply to walk part of the way to work or to the shops, you will be building valuable exercise into your day. Walking gives you 'space' – time to make the adjustment between work and home, or time to think through a problem. If you rely on a car or public transport, consider parking the car just a bit further away, or getting off a stop early or a stop late.

How many calories you can burn up by walking will depend, among other things, on how quickly you walk. I suggest either 30 minutes' brisk walking, or 45 minutes at a more moderate pace, three or four times each week.

Cycling

Like walking, cycling is a very practical form of exercise. You may be able to cycle to work or college or to the shops; or if you can't use it as a way of getting around, you could use it for relaxing and exploring the countryside at weekends or on holiday. Cycling is 'green' – by choosing to cycle instead of taking the car you are helping to reduce pollution. Once you have a bike it's cheap – if you want to experiment, try hiring one for a while. Cycling can help to build up your endurance – and will also help to strengthen your leg muscles. You could also try using a stationary exercise bike. You can stop whenever you want without being stuck miles from home, and you can just about watch TV at the same time . . .

To help you stay slim without smoking, you need to cycle three or four times a week at a moderate pace for around 20 minutes, or at a more gentle pace for around half an hour – say on the way to work – or go for a much longer cycle ride with friends at the weekend.

SENSIBLE PRECAUTIONS

Don't exercise if you have a cold, sore throat or a temperature, and stop if you feel dizzy, in pain, sick or unusually fatigued.

If you have a history of chest pains, high blood pressure, heart disease, asthma, bronchitis, or diabetes, if you are obese (see page 42), or if you are recovering from an operation, you should consult your family doctor before you embark on an exercise plan. Exercise may be recommended, but it should be medically supervised.

Jogging and Running

These are the last of the exercises which can be used as a way of getting from A to B – although if you want to jog to work or college you may need to persuade someone to install some showers!

Like all sports, jogging has its enthusiasts; it also has its critics. The enthusiasts can be seen every day jogging or, if they are more energetic, running, round parks all over the world, from Hyde Park to Central Park to the Auckland Domain – and taking part in charity fun runs and half-marathons galore. The critics are keen to point out that jogging can harm your joints (which is true if the proper precautions aren't followed); that people have died jogging (which is also true) and that people get more exercise going to the funerals of people who have died jogging than did the joggers themselves (which is not true).

On the plus side, jogging can be done anywhere, anytime, and requires little equipment beyond a good pair of running shoes, T-shirt and shorts and a track suit for cold days. It can be done alone, or with others – if you're just starting out you will get a lot of encouragement by joining a local club where you will find other people to keep your motivation high. On the minus side, jogging does put a lot of pressure on weight-bearing joints, especially if you have no choice but to pound along a hard surface – so it isn't a good choice for people who are overweight. A good pair of running shoes is essential – the sole should be well-cushioned, especially at the heel, and there should be plenty of support for the arch of your foot.

The other reason why jogging has attracted adverse publicity has to do with the so-called 'jogger's high' – or the tendency of some joggers to become 'addicted' to jogging. Certainly there are recorded instances of people who jog, run or take other forms of exercise to excess. As with anything, you can have too much of a good thing – regular exercise most days is fine, but if you reach the point where you must exercise at all costs, then it has gone too far. You have to let good sense prevail.

To help you stay slim without smoking, I suggest jogging three or four times a week at a slow pace for a good half hour – twenty minutes if you can build up to a moderate pace.

Swimming

I add this because it is the best all-round form of activity – it gives you stamina, strengthens the muscles of your legs and arms and helps to keep you supple. It is at once exhilarating and relaxing, invigorating and calming; and as the water lends you its own support, it's ideal if you are overweight. Sadly, many overweight people are afraid to strip down to a swimming costume, only too well aware that they do not have the sort of figure they see in advertisements. Having summoned up the courage to do so, they are often rewarded at last by the realization that hardly anyone else does either. Instead they meet women and men who are preoccupied not with outer appearance but with inner fitness and health. For this reason, if for no other, swimming can be a great source of relief and motivation for the would-be quitter. Its only drawback is a practical one. To swim regularly you need to live or work within striking distance of a pool and you have to *make* the time to fit a swim into your day. It's worth exploring your options – some pools open for early sessions and stay open late; some operate creches; many operate single sex sessions and run classes for all level of swimmers – even complete beginners.

To help you stay slim without smoking, I suggest swimming at a moderate pace for around half an hour, three or four times a week. Or 'mix and match'. Try swimming on some days and walking on others.

EXERCISE FOR PEOPLE WHO HATE EXERCISE

Finally let's admit that taking exercise isn't everyone's cup of tea. If you've tried it, and really don't want to pursue it, or if you simply can't make the time, then try looking for lots of small lifestyle changes instead. In other words, *do what you normally do, but do it a bit more energetically*: take the stairs instead of the lift; walk to the post box instead of taking the car; avoid driving round and round the supermarket car park trying to find the space nearest the entrance; stand instead of sitting; get up when you need to reach something instead of stretching over; join in with your children's games – as many 'hidden' changes as you can think of. Small changes *count*. How many extra calories you could burn up this way, and how much benefit to your health and well-being, will depend on exactly how many changes you make – but you could easily clock up enough extra exercise to help you stay slim without smoking.

Getting Started

Start gradually, work up to your target slowly, and don't expect too much of yourself, too quickly. Don't assume that you are fit just because you occasionally manage to sprint for the bus – this doesn't mean that you will be able to endure vigorous aerobic exercise for long. You need to get fit to play fast sports (like squash), not play fast sports to get fit. So if exercise is new to you, start out by walking for, say, 15 minutes a day and gradually build up your speed and the length of time you walk for. Then, if you want, try something more energetic.

Don't expect to make progress at a steady rate. You are far more likely to reach a plateau where you stay for some time, before you feel able to push yourself further. Ideally – if you want to achieve the protective effect against heart disease – you need to exercise several times a week, and quite vigorously. As a rule of thumb, the exercise should feel somewhere between 'fairly hard' and 'hard' but never painful – brisk walking is ideal. Above all, don't push yourself too hard, and drive yourself away from what you're trying to achieve because of exhaustion. You might enjoy keeping a 'fitness diary'. Make a note of when you exercise, and for how long, how easy or difficult you found it, and how you felt afterwards.

Planning Ahead

Use this section of the book to write down the types of exercise you plan to do when you quit smoking. Make a note of the ones you are definitely going to do, and the ones which you might try out now or later.

Think about the practicalities of your choice. How regularly will you be able to exercise? Do you plan to exercise with a friend? What kind of arrangements will you have to make to put your plan into action?

Type of Exercise	How Many Times a Week	How Long (Target)

6

THINKING ABOUT QUITTING

'Smoking is like a lousy love affair: you hate the man, but you can't let him go.'

Participant on
Five Day Plan to Stop Smoking
April 1987

You have to want to quit smoking to succeed. Obviously you want to quit smoking, or you wouldn't be reading this book, but you have to want to quit smoking very much indeed. This is not to say that it will be difficult, but that it will be easier if you have convinced yourself that you want to be rid of it once and for all.

Now you would be unusual if at this point you did not start to experience some doubt about your commitment to the whole idea. There are very, very few smokers who smoke for one reason and one reason only, such as staying slim, even if it is their *main* reason, and knowing how to get over this particular hurdle may not be the whole story. Most smokers have a love/hate relationship with their smoking. They want to stop smoking, but they just can't bring themselves to let go.

But isn't it all just a question of willpower? The answer to this question is **no**. It is not just a question of willpower. In fact, it is not really a question of willpower at all. Now this may surprise you; most people believe that you need a lot of willpower to stop smoking. But willpower is a loaded concept.

Just think about it:

If you need a lot of willpower to stop smoking (as many authors will lead you to believe) then it follows that stopping smoking must be very difficult.

↓

If stopping smoking is so difficult, then are you sure you can succeed?

↓

If you are not sure you can succeed, then you are more likely to fail, because confidence is a prerequisite for success

↓

And if you do fail, whose fault will it be? Your fault? Or mine, for making it sound too easy?

↓

Yours of course, for being weak-willed and unable to make your own decisions.

This is what's known as blaming the victim. But if willpower is not the key to stopping smoking, then what is? If there is a key, it is 'wantpower'. It depends upon the balance of 'pros' and 'cons'. The 'cons', you know about already – the costs of smoking – both social and financial, and the health risks. I doubt if you'll need much convincing that they exist, although you may well *underestimate* them. But what about the 'pros' – the things which keep you smoking?

From the Cradle to the Grave

The first question to ask yourself is what made you start smoking in the first place? Many of your beliefs about smoking probably predate your first cigarette, and although your attitudes will have changed over the years, you are unlikely to have shrugged off your earliest perceptions of what it means to be 'a smoker'. So cast your mind back to the time before you took your first cigarette. What, or who, motivated you to start smoking and why?

_____

_____

_____

_____

_____

Answers vary, but some crop up time and time again.

There are the *social reasons*: 'Everyone was doing it'; 'It helped me to feel part of the crowd'; 'It was a way of breaking the ice'; 'It gave me something to do with my hands'; 'I thought smoking would help me to look glamorous and sophisticated'.

There's *rebellion*: 'I had my first cigarette behind the bike-shed'; 'Smoking was the forbidden fruit – of course, that made us do it all the more'; 'We used to stand just outside the school gates smoking a cigarette'.

And there's *need*: 'I thought smoking would help me to lose weight'; 'I was studying for my exams at the time – I thought smoking would help me concentrate'; 'At the funeral, someone just handed me a cigarette, to calm me down'; 'I thought it would help me get over a difficult period'.

Where do these views spring from? One clue is that smoking habits tend to be passed down through families. Children are more likely to smoke if their parents smoke, especially if both of them do. The little girl who watches her mother light up a cigarette whenever things get tense is likely to grow up believing that smoking helps people to relax. The teenager who watches his father chain-smoke as he pores over a difficult piece of work will naturally assume that smoking helps people to concentrate. Almost by definition, a child who watches her parents smoke, when she herself is not allowed to do so, will view smoking as a sign of adulthood. The fact that they deplore smoking is hardly a deterrent – if smoking is so dangerous (the child reasons) but they carry on doing it anyway, then it must have something really going for it! Children are more likely to smoke if their elder brother or sister is a smoker, and more likely to smoke if their friends are smokers too.

This idea – that attitudes about smoking are passed down from generation to generation and peer group to peer group – goes some way to explaining what people believe about smoking, but it's not the whole story. Few people nowadays view smoking as alluring or sophisticated, but where on earth did we get the idea in the first place? After all, it's difficult to believe that there is anything intrinsically attractive about sticking a tube of paper and dried-up leaf in your mouth, setting fire to the end and breathing in the fumes.

The answer must surely be the media. Just as the tobacco industry went out of its way to convince us that smoking could make us slim, so too has it gone out of its way to convince us that smoking goes hand in hand with:

> affluence
> social mobility
> or working-class solidarity,
>
> emancipation
> or subordination,
> rugged charm
> or feminine chic,
>
> creativity, concentration
> or relaxation,
>
> romance, modesty
> or sexual success,
>
> and health, fitness & vitality . . .

Over the years, models and high society figures have been paid to smoke under the glare of the camera; actors, actresses, even doctors have been invited to testify that they smoke this or that brand of cigarette; film producers have been persuaded to have their actors smoke on screen; and billions of pounds and dollars have been invested in advertising, and sponsorship of sport and the arts. Governments may have intervened more or less determinedly to restrict such practices but the images embraced by them live on. In theatre, in films, in novels and in television, smoking is used to convey the sense of the moment: the actor who lights up to fill a dramatic pause, the wounded soldier who is offered a cigarette, the spy who chain-smokes through an encounter in the East; the soap-opera star who smokes to relieve the boredom of the day; the shared cigarette after sex.

What it all adds up to is an *image* of what smoking is and what it can do for you. Some of it is obvious nonsense (smoking does not make you wealthy, much less healthy), but what about the rest of it?

Recall, for a moment, your first cigarette. It may have symbolized the thrill of adulthood, but would you claim that you felt any immediate benefits? Few people do. Most people say that their first cigarette 'tasted awful' or 'made me feel sick and dizzy' and recall that they had to learn to inhale, even though 'it hurt to begin with'. Novice smokers do not go through with this for the hell of it: they go through it because they have grown up to believe that smoking is a good thing to do.

Probably the first 'advantage' of smoking that most of us experience is a social one: cigarettes may be a passport to a particular group of friends who gather together to smoke at parties, at the pub or behind the bike sheds. The pleasure of social smoking has of course little to do with the pleasure of smoking itself; it is mostly hype. Thirty or forty years ago, smoking was all the rage, nowadays, smoking is more 'out' than 'in'.

What about the other 'advantages' of smoking: relaxation, concentration, coping with stress, for example? Oddly enough, these tend to be realized at just about the same time that the smoker begins to realize something else: it is no longer so easy to manage without smoking. In other words, they are hooked.

Now to begin with, most smokers resist this idea. 'I can quit smoking at any time – but I just don't want to at the moment,' 'I don't smoke much – and anyway, I enjoy it' and so on. In fact, it often takes quite a bizarre occurrence to bring home to the smoker that he or she is addicted to cigarettes. One smoker told me that the truth only dawned upon him when he booked a non-smoking seat on a flight to the USA. Two hours into the flight, he asked an air hostess if he could be transferred to a smoking seat. Only when he heard the request for a swap go out over the tannoy did he finally accept that truth: he was well and truly hooked.

But what does it mean to be addicted? Few people make the connection between tobacco and hard drugs, because there isn't the same social stigma attached, but tobacco is one of the most addictive substances known to humanity. Think of what you know about addiction to hard drugs. To begin with, the user gets a 'high' out of a fix, but after a while, *tolerance* sets in. The body becomes less and less sensitive to the drug, and the user needs to take more and more in order to get an effect. After a while *withdrawal* sets in. The user no longer gets much of a 'high' from a fix, but they feel terrible without one, which is to say that they experience *withdrawal effects* if they do not get their fix. Being addicted means that they have to keep on taking the drug just to feel normal. Now, you do not get the same sort of 'high' from smoking, nor are the withdrawal symptoms anything like as bad (some people barely experience them at all), but the idea is the same.

Nicotine is a very fast acting drug. Every time you smoke a cigarette, the levels of nicotine in your brain rise quickly to a peak and then begin to fall. If you are addicted to nicotine, a feeling of discomfort will begin to set in, so that you feel the need for a cigarette to relieve the withdrawal effects. It is not so much that smoking a cigarette makes the smoker feel better: rather that the cigarette stops them feeling worse.

In his excellent book, Allen Carr puts it like this[1]

'Smoking is like wearing tight shoes just to obtain the pleasure you feel when taking them off. The reason that smokers cannot see it that way is twofold.

1. There is no physical pain which we can identify. It is just a feeling.

2. It happens in reverse . . . When you light up you obtain relief – so you are fooled into believing the cigarette is some sort of pleasure or prop.'

Mr Carr probably stretches the point too far. I don't wish to suggest that all of the so-called 'advantages' of smoking are 'withdrawal relief'. The scientific evidence simply doesn't exist to prove the point one way or the other. But withdrawal relief plays a part. And the illusion created is a powerful one. Most smokers become addicted to nicotine to a greater or lesser extent, and the lucky few who don't, learn much about the 'advantages' of smoking from those who do. So – one way or the other most smokers become hooked to their smoking: *physically, mentally or both*. And it is this which keeps them smoking.

[1] from: *The Easy Way to Stop Smoking*, pp 16-17, Penguin Books, London, 1987, copyright © Allen Carr, 1985. Reproduced by kind permission of Penguin Books Ltd.:

Smoking and Anger

Doubtful? Imagine the following situation. Your partner has just arrived home after a lousy day. You've had a bad day too. Tempers flare and you get into an argument. After about 20 minutes you've had enough and storm out. It is now over an hour since you last had a cigarette. You take one out of its packet and light up. The cigarette calms you down. You go back inside and soon after manage to patch up your differences. You reach the obvious conclusion. Smoking helps to calm you down. Your 14-year-old daughter, not yet a smoker, has observed the whole scenario and draws the same conclusion: smoking helps to calm you down. Everything which you had both been led to believe about smoking, through advertising, books, films etc., is confirmed.

But hang on.

Did smoking *actually* help to calm you down, or did it simply relieve the feeling of tension which was already setting in because you had not had a cigarette for some time? Did you need the cigarette to calm you down, or did you need it to relieve the withdrawal symptoms caused by the last cigarette?

Smoking and Stress

The same kind of problem crops up with smoking and stress. Many people smoke more when they are under stress, but this doesn't prove that smoking helps them to cope. There are two schools of thought. Some scientists believe that smoking can help people to deal with stressful situations because it can help them relax or deal with problems. Others argue that we become tolerant to these effects, so it's mainly withdrawal relief which counts. Given a stressful situation, the smoker is in double trouble, because the longer they go without smoking, the worse they feel. When eventually they do take a cigarette, the total amount of stress they were feeling at the time is reduced – creating the illusion that smoking has helped them to cope. One ex-smoker, a TV producer, put it like this:

'When I was a smoker, life just seemed to be one stressful situation after another. Whenever a problem blew up, I vanished behind a cloud of smoke. I would be on the telephone smoking cigarette after cigarette, or yelling at the production team. I thought that smoking helped to calm me down: everyone else thought I looked like a nervous wreck. What smoking *actually* did was take my mind off the situation so that I didn't realize that I wasn't doing anything to solve it. When I finally quit, I discovered a whole range of new ways of dealing with problems, and if anything I now cope even better than before. *Smoking was not so much a way of coping, as a way of not coping'.*

In fact there is no evidence at all that stopping smoking reduces people's long-term ability to deal with stress. To begin with, the new ex-smoker may feel anxious or irritable or even angry, but these are withdrawal symptoms and they do not last. Long term, ex-smokers say they cope just as well as they did when they smoked, or better. They often report a tremendous sense of well-being and self-confidence and say they feel better able to tackle life, not worse.

Smoking on the Job

If smoking does not help people to cope with stress, then what about coping with work? Perhaps you feel that you need to smoke in order to concentrate on your job, or that smoking helps you to be creative? Perhaps you genuinely fear that you will never again be able to do a decent day's work if you quit smoking, and that you will put your entire career and future on the line. But once again, we have to ask the question – does smoking really help people to work, or does their addiction mean that they cannot work without smoking? Withdrawal relief is an important part of it, because the last thing you need when you are trying to do something difficult is a distraction like the discomfort of not smoking. Most people begin a really difficult task by getting other minor problems out of the way, and lighting a cigarette is just part of the process. As for the possibility that smoking can actually *improve* performance, the evidence, to date, is weak. On the one hand, there is evidence that nicotine can help people to sustain attention on simple tasks, but on the other, there is evidence that smoking can impair memory. As solving a problem usually involves both, the net effect can by no means be guaranteed to help. As one history lecturer explained:

'In my smoking days, I used to sit up half the night working on my book. I felt I could concentrate for ages, and that I was really homing in on the problem, but on the other hand, I found it quite difficult to get my thoughts down on paper.

When I first quit I wondered whether I would ever be able to write again, but this soon passed. Looking back, I now realize that it was a question of swings and roundabouts. What I gained on the concentration front, I lost on the memory front, because I kept having to go back over the section I'd just read and I couldn't make the connection between one idea and another. Nowadays, I get the same amount of work done, but it doesn't take me nearly as long.'

In fact, it is difficult to believe that smoking is crucial to people's ability to do their work when you look at the people who are most likely to have quit: doctors and professional people from all walks of life with responsible and demanding jobs. Where is the evidence that their ability to do their jobs has fallen apart?

The Boredom Cigarette

So – like the stress cigarette, the concentration cigarette is an illusion. But what about smoking when you are bored? Perhaps you smoke when you have nothing else to do and are wondering how you will fill the time. Still, it is difficult to understand why. A smoker can spend a whole evening 'just smoking'. It takes just a few seconds to light a cigarette, and perhaps you spend a few seconds more just watching the smoke curling and drifting away. But what do you do for the rest of the time? Perhaps the cigarette gives you something to do with your hands – but there must be more to smoking than just that or you could make do with a pencil. Isn't part of the reason really withdrawal relief? When you are busy you probably don't notice that slight feeling of discomfort which begins to set in soon after the last cigarette has worn off. Not so when you are bored. Part of the reason why people smoke when they are bored is not because smoking is interesting, but because being bored reminds them that they are not smoking. As one teenager pointed out, this often means doing absolutely nothing at all:

> 'There were always parties on in the evening – and most of the time, you just drifted from one to another. Some of them were really great, but quite often I spent most of the evening just propping up the bar and smoking just one cigarette after another. Every time I was about to go home, I'd smoke just one more cigarette, just to make me feel better. The first time I went to a party after I'd quit smoking I realized that it was just dead boring. So, instead of hanging around smoking and wasting my money on drinks, I went home and rang a friend'.

Smoking is not a way of dealing with boredom, but a way of not dealing with it. Smoking can make you feel tired and lethargic so that you cannot be bothered to do anything else. Not only can it shorten life, it wastes it.

The Pleasure of Smoking

Finally, addiction can masquerade in mysterious ways. Just think of the times which people say they really enjoy a cigarette. Take the first cigarette of the day. Many smokers say that this one is special. But the fact is that after a night-time without cigarettes, nicotine levels hit rock bottom. Tolerance is low and withdrawal is high. It's not magic, but the power of addiction – the same power of addiction which leads smokers to brave the crush in the theatre bar during the interval, or to rush out in the middle of the night to buy cigarettes, or to go to considerable extremes to avoid ever running out at all.

Much the same goes for the cigarette after meals. Most smokers regard this as a question of habit; they also say they enjoy it. But it's not that simple. Many heavy smokers positively dread invitations to dinner with a bunch of non-smokers. The smoker who likes to smoke between courses is the prime example. She cannot wait for the meal to be over so she can smoke: does she 'enjoy' her cigarette or does the need to smoke mean she cannot 'enjoy' her meal?

Lifeskills

I hope I have sown the seed of doubt about some of the so-called 'advantages' of smoking. Just as you do not need to smoke to be slim, so you do not need to smoke to cope, to relax, or enjoy yourself. There are far better ways of doing all these things. In the next chapter, I want to show you how.

7

LIFESKILLS

'A really busy man never knows how much he weighs'

Edgar Watson Howe
Country Towns Sayings 1911

'Mr Howard Saxby, literary agent, was knitting a sock. He knitted a great deal, he would tell you if you asked, to keep himself from smoking, adding that he also smoked a good deal to keep himself from knitting.'

P G Wodehouse
Cocktail Time, 1958

Out of the Fire . . .
And Into the Frying Pan?

Some people view smoking and eating as two sides of the same coin. They fear that if they break their addiction to cigarettes, they will end up addicted to food, and so become fat. This is untrue. As we have seen, not everyone who stops smoking gains weight, and most of those who do, do not gain much. So it isn't a universal problem. There is no reason to anticipate a sudden loss of control over your eating, and stopping smoking should not make you fat.

But the idea raises some fascinating questions. Smoking is addictive, but is it also possible to become addicted to food? Are problems with smoking and problems with eating really similar – or are they quite different? And what can we learn from smoking 'therapy' which might help us to avoid overeating, or vice-versa?

What Do We Mean by Addiction?

Scientists define addiction in a very precise way. If you want to say that something is 'addictive' it has to measure up to a set of carefully defined criteria. Tobacco fits them very well. Most people who smoke tobacco do so on a regular basis: around 1 out of every 3 children who experiment with cigarettes goes on to become a smoker in adult life, and of these, around 90 per cent will smoke on a regular controlled basis. Tobacco contains nicotine, a mood-altering substance, which is believed to be responsible for its addictive power, and – and this is a clincher – giving people nicotine brings about a dose-related decrease in cigarette consumption.

But what about food? Some people think they are addicted to food because they sometimes find themselves overwhelmed by an uncontrollable or *compulsive* desire to eat – even when they don't want to. People smoke compulsively too (as if to punish themselves for continuing to smoke when they want to quit), but this isn't sufficient to have it labelled an addiction. In other respects, eating falls far short of the mark. We all have to eat, but although compulsive eating is common, it is by no means inevitable. Surveys show that only around a quarter of women (and a much smaller percentage of men) experience regular episodes of uncontrolled or 'binge eating', and even then, many of them control their eating sufficiently to avoid getting fat. There is no single substance in food which has ever been shown to be responsible for its 'addictive' power. True, a case is sometimes made, for example, for sugar, or phenyl-ethylamine in chocolate, but a more likely explanation is that eating foods we like simply whets the appetite for more. Eating is not an addiction, so it's impossible to swap an addiction to cigarettes for an 'addiction' to food.

Dependency and Habit

But problems with smoking and eating do have their similarities. As we've seen, smokers often smoke in response to underlying situations – like stress or boredom, if only because not smoking makes the situation worse. Rachel, who we met in chapter 2 (page 30), smoked to help her over the problems of being a single parent, and even though she wanted to quit, she felt *dependent* on her cigarettes to get her through the day. She was also aware that she smoked in response to specific 'cues' which she had come to link, through force of habit, with her smoking. Take drinking for example. To begin she used to have a cigarette with a drink, just because it is (actually, *was*) the thing to do, but as the years went by it became a habit. She reached a point where she found it difficult to have a drink *without* a cigarette, simply because she'd been doing it for so long. You'll hear more about this in the next chapter, when we come to look at ways of avoiding your own smoking 'cues'.

If you've ever experienced a problem with eating or staying slim, you'll recognize some parallels here. Eating can be a source of comfort and reward. Many parents unwittingly use food as a universal pacifier when their children are young, and in adult life many of us feel tempted to turn to food when times are tough. People also get into the habit of eating in response to external cues – while they're watching TV or reading a book, or just because they happen to be passing the fridge – (which is one of the reasons why I recommended that you stick to a regular meal pattern). In fact, if you talk to people who find it difficult to stay slim, you'll find that they frequently eat in the situations that other people smoke:

- when they are sad
- when they are lonely
- when they want to enjoy themselves
- when they are worried
- when they are angry or frustrated
- when they feel there is something missing
- when they feel they have failed
- when they are too bored to do anything else
- when they are trying to put off doing something else
- when they are trying to work through a difficult problem and
- when they are trying to comfort themselves for eating 'too much'

A Subtle Illusion

What makes the situation even worse is that neither smoking nor eating really help. We've already seen how many of the so-called advantages of smoking are really an illusion created by the addictive power of cigarettes, but has it ever struck you that smoking is *itself* very stressful? If someone told you that you should combat stress by taking a pill which put up your heart rate and blood pressure, and also doubled your risk of death, you would think them quite mad. Yet this is precisely what you are doing by smoking. And now that the smoking tide has turned, many smokers find themselves left out in the cold – which can add further stress to an already stressful situation. Both Rachel and Clare (page 34) saw through this. They were worried about their smoking and they wanted to stop, but they were locked into a vicious cycle. The worse they felt about their smoking, the less they felt able to break free. Much the same is true of comfort eating. Treating yourself to the occasional bar of chocolate when you feel down will probably do more good than harm, but if it becomes a habit, it can spell disaster. Far from helping to solve problems, it can create a new one (obesity) which can become more important than the original one which caused it. People who eat compulsively are rarely in doubt about this; a binge may provide temporary solace, but all too often it is followed by remorse and guilt.

The fact is that many people cope with problems despite smoking and food, and not because of it. What can make it difficult for them to quit is not that they are any worse off, but that without cigarettes or food to distract them, they feel exposed.

It is not only smokers who face problems. The difference is that non-smokers have had the chance over the years to build up their own familiar ways of dealing with them.

How to Kill Two Birds with One Stone

All of this means that some of the strategies which can help people to stop smoking, can also help people who want to overcome an eating problem – or people who want to avoid one ever developing. I call these strategies Lifeskills, because this is what they are. You can use them to help you become a slim ex-smoker, but you can also use them to help with problems in other areas of your life. But let's be clear about it. We're not talking about mere alternatives to smoking or eating – which don't really help, but about really constructive ways of dealing with problems. Use them – and you will be *better* equipped to deal with life than ever before.

This makes them sound very exciting. But they're not. Lifeskills are not miracle solutions to life, death and the universe – but rather basic, commonsense problem-solving skills which you have to master for yourself. But they work, and you can get them to work for you. It's up to you to find out which ones will suit, in which situations.

RELAXATION SKILLS

In many people's opinion, exercise and relaxation are the opposite of each other. This is true, but only up to a point. As we've seen, exercising can actually help you to feel relaxed (afterwards), whereas what most of us really mean by 'relaxing' isn't really relaxing at all. Just because we are slumped in front of the TV at the end of the day, with a cigarette in one hand and a drink in the other, doesn't mean we are relaxed: most of the muscles in our body will still be tightened up from the stresses and strains of the day.

Relaxation is a skill, and a very powerful one at that. Knowing how to relax can help you deal constructively with anxiety, so that you won't feel the need to turn to cigarettes or food. But you need to learn how – right from square one. Think of it like learning to ride a bicycle. In time it will come effortlessly, and you'll be able to relax whenever you want to. But to begin with you need to work at it. There are many kinds of relaxation skills – I want to show you just two. If you find it difficult to do them on your own, I recommend using a relaxation tape (cassette), to guide you through. They're widely available in bookshops.

Tense and Relax

The purpose of this training is to allow you to become deeply relaxed – perhaps more deeply than ever before. I want to help you to recognize feelings of tension in your muscles, and to know how to let the tension go.

To practise this skill, you need to set aside half an

hour in a quiet place, where you won't be disturbed. Lie down, or sit comfortably, in comfortable clothing and without shoes. To begin with, you are going to learn to clench and relax sixteen muscle groups. Once you get the hang of it, you won't need to work on so many.

We'll start with your hand and forearm. First tense the muscles in your right hand, and lower right arm, by making a tight fist. Feel the tension in your hand, over your knuckles, and up your lower arm. Feel the tension. Now let it go. Not gradually, but immediately. Let all the tension go at once.

Now move to the muscles in your upper right arm. Tense these muscles by pushing your elbow down against the arm of your chair. You should feel tension in your upper arm, but still feel relaxed in your lower arm. Feel the tension. Now let it go.

Now that you have relaxed the muscles in your right hand and arm, move over to your left arm. Tense and relax the muscles in the left arm just as you did on the right.

Now move on to your face and neck. First tense the muscles in the upper part of your face by raising your eyebrows as high as you can, so that you can feel the tension in your scalp. Feel the tension. Now let it go.

Next, tense the muscles in the middle of your face. Screw up your eyes very tightly and wrinkle up your nose. Feel the tension. Now let it go.

Move on to the lower part of your face. Clench your teeth and pull back the corners of your mouth, so that you can feel the tension right back to your jaw. Feel the tension. Now let it go.

Go on to your neck muscles. Pull your chin downwards towards your chest, and at the same time pull your chest backwards so the chin doesn't touch it. Feel the tension. Now let it go.

Now move on to the muscles in your chest, shoulders and upper back. You can tense several muscles together. Take a deep breath and hold it, and at the same time pull back your shoulders, as if to make your shoulder blades touch. Feel the tension in your neck, your shoulders and your back. Now let it go.

Now that you have relaxed your upper body, move to the muscles in your abdomen (tummy). Tense up your stomach as hard as you can, as if someone was about to punch you there. Feel the tension. Now let it go. Now move to your legs and feet. Begin by tensing the muscles in your right thigh. The big muscle on the top of your leg should feel quite hard. Feel the tension. Now let it go.

Move on to the right calf. Tense the muscles by pulling your toes upwards towards your head, so that you can feel the tension spreading through your calf. Feel the tension. Now let it go. Now move on to your right foot. Point your foot inwards and curl your toes at the same time. Feel the tension throughout the arch and ball of your foot. Feel the tension. Now let it go.

Go on to the muscles in your left leg and foot. Tense and relax them exactly as you did with the right leg. Feel the tension. Now let it go.

Having worked through all sixteen muscle groups, make sure that you can't feel any tightness or tension anywhere. Focus on each group of muscles separately in the order you worked through them. Notice where the tension is, and what it feels like. Remember what it felt like when you let the tension go. Now move on the next muscle group and so on, until your whole body feels deeply, deeply relaxed.

Practice this skill often – at least once a day. In time you will be able to abandon the tensing procedure altogether, and go straight into relaxing.

Don't be put off by its simplicity. Properly mastered, it has been shown to reduce blood pressure in hypertensive patients. Hypertension (high blood pressure) is a major risk factor for a heart attack. It may be simple, but it works.

Breathing and Relaxation Combined

This is another powerful skill. Sit comfortably or lie down, in a quiet place, where you will be undisturbed for at least twenty minutes.

I want you to think about your breathing. Imagine that you are very tense or worked up about something. Notice how your breathing becomes quick and shallow, not slow and deep. Take a quick deep breath. Notice whether your abdomen (tummy) is pulled in sharply or whether it expands.

Now concentrate on making your breathing as relaxed as possible. Breathe in and out, slowly and rhythmically. Breathe in through your nose, and out through your mouth. Notice your abdomen expanding as you breathe in. Carry on just breathing in and out, in and out. Don't force it. Make it gentle and even, slow and rhythmical. Concentrate on each breath, in and out, in and out.

Now start to relax your muscles, working through them in the same order as you did in the 'tensing and relaxing' exercise. You don't need to tense them first, just make sure that you have let all the tension go. Start with your lower right arm and hand, and simply by thinking about it, let the tension go. Now move on to the rest of your arm, and simply by thinking about it, let the tension go. Carry on like this until you feel completely relaxed throughout your body – the whole process should take about ten minutes.

Now just concentrate on your breathing. Notice the flow of your breath. In and out. In and out. Stay like this for as long as you like, just enjoying the feeling of deep relaxation.

Practise this often. In time you will be able to do it anywhere, any time – in the car, on the bus, sitting at your desk or on the sofa. Use it as a way of calming yourself, so that feelings of anxiety and tension can't build up.

MANAGING STRESS

So – we've looked at one way of coping with stress – but why on earth does the stress arise in the first place? What do we mean by 'stress' – and why is it now, in the late 20th century, that we've come to hear so much about it? Critics of the 'stress' culture are fond of pointing out that life today is by no means as stressful as it used to be. By implication, they argue, the entire 'stress business' must be a fad.

But it's not that simple. True, few of us now live in

the kind of poverty and hardship which once was common, nor do many of us have to fear for our lives every time we step out of our door. Today's stresses rarely take the shape of a physical threat, but they are no less real to us because of it. What makes a situation stressful is not the situation itself, but the way we view it, and the way we deal with it.

'Stress' can affect us at many levels: unemployment; or the fear of unemployment; a drop in income and poor housing; the frustration of poor transport and pollution; difficulty in achieving in an achievement-oriented society; difficulty with juggling the conflicting demands of career and family; difficulty with stopping smoking and staying slim. And so on. Some of us are so busy that we never have the time to deal with problems, and some of us have so much time that we end up turning them endlessly over and over in our minds. Either way, we don't make much progress.

So – if stress is a problem, start by thinking about the sources of stress in your life. Take your time – ideally, by keeping a record over a week or two. Note down the stresses which occur regularly, paying particular attention to the times when you automatically light up a cigarette in response (or decide to eat instead). If you want, you can keep a 'stress diary' – along the lines of the food diary shown on page 58. Now take a long hard look.

Sorting Things Out

First, see if you can actually eliminate some of the problems. Does it have to be you who does the school run every morning or the washing up every night? Do you really have time to babysit for the next-door neighbour – or are you actually spreading yourself too thin? Are you really indispensable?

If you can't actually eliminate problems, can you modify them? Do you really have to cook from scratch every night? (You can still eat well and conveniently.) If travelling in the rush hour is driving you mad, could you travel a bit earlier, or later – even if does mean less time at home?

If changing matters for the better has to involve other people, then ask yourself whether it's reasonable or realistic to ask them. If it is, then do so as *assertively* as possible. Simply explain, without elaboration, that you haven't got the time, or that you need their support. You don't need to be aggressive about it, even if you do feel that they are the cause of your problem in the first place. An assertive approach is much more likely to be met with respect and a positive response, than is an aggressive or angry one.

What you're left with is the stress which you have to cope with. It doesn't make much sense to spend a great deal of time and effort organizing your life so that nothing goes wrong. Stress is inevitable, and your effort will be far better invested in developing a battery of skills to help you deal with it. Nor is it usually helpful to deal with stressful situations by shying away from them. Sometimes this kind of coping *can* help, if you need to get through a few very difficult or sad days, but sooner or later problems have to be dealt with head on.

Breaking Things Down

Looking in depth at problems often helps people to see that they are not insurmountable. Sometimes it's a question of organization: breaking the problem down into a series of small, manageable steps. We've seen this in action already when we looked in chapter 4 at ways of dealing with an eating 'problem' – but the approach can work well in other settings. Perhaps you're being held back at work by lack of a particular skill (what would you have to do to get it?) – or at home where problems tend to pile up on top of one another, because the one which takes longest gets left until last?

Thinking Things Through

But if all this sounds too simplistic, it may be because the stresses in your life can't be resolved this way. Very often the real problem is not the task itself – a report to be written, a difficult phone call to be made or an awkward topic to be raised – but the way we feel about it. Becoming overanxious about things is very self-defeating, and it's guaranteed to undermine our ability to achieve whatever we have to. It tends to focus our minds on the dreadful consequences of what might happen if . . . or on the reasons behind it, all of which distracts our attention from finding a solution in the here and now.

Even if the situation is insoluble – the loss of a loved one, for example, very often it's the way we *feel* about it which makes the difference between coping or not. Being able to relax when we feel anxiety welling up can be very helpful indeed, but you may also find it helpful to tackle the thinking which lies behind the threat. Our thoughts are very powerful. In those private conversations which we have in our heads, between 'us and ourself', we think about what we're doing, what we might have done, what we're going to do next, whether we're going to be able to do it and so on.

What's the Worst Which Can Happen?

This is an approach which is especially popular in my family. I've used it throughout my life. Whenever someone is worried about something, somebody else always asks – what's the worst which could happen? It usually turns out that even the worst outcome would be bearable, if by no means ideal. 'What if the house isn't spotlessly clean every day?' 'What if your application for college is refused?' 'What if your partner loses his job?' Most problems are worse in the thinking than in the doing. Replacing the irrational thought that 'such and such mustn't happen at all costs' with the thought that 'I don't want it to happen, but it may happen, and if it does I'll handle it' may not change anything – but it may help you to cope.

IRRATIONAL THINKING

A lot of irrational thinking goes on in our heads. It can get in the way of our ability to stop smoking, stay slim or lose weight. And it can hold us back from tackling some of the underlying problems too. Look at these examples:

Black and White Thinking

Laura wants to lose weight and has put herself on a strict diet. All goes well until, in a moment of temptation, she cuts a sliver of the cake left over from her son's birthday party. Most people would have done the same, but she doesn't see it that way. 'I'm a complete failure,' she tells herself. 'I've got no self-control,' she says. This makes her feel guilty. She abandons the attempt to lose weight, and finds herself right back at square one.

Global Thinking

Chris is turned down for a job which she very much wanted. The truth is that jobs are scarce, that there were hundreds of applicants, and anyway the job was always going to go to the internal candidate. But she doesn't see it that way. 'I made a mess of answering the questions,' she tells herself. 'I'm useless,' she says, 'I'll never get a job'. For days, she can't even face looking at the job ads, and when she does finally get to another interview, she's so anxious about being rejected that she doesn't come across as well as she might. In the meantime she consoles herself by smoking – 'I'm too stressed to quit,' she tells herself, so adding to her sense of failure and despair.

Dwelling On the Past

Caroline is about to embark upon another attempt to quit smoking. She's tried before and failed. This isn't surprising, as it often takes more than one attempt. But she doesn't see it that way. 'I wasn't able to manage it last time,' she tells herself. 'So, I'll probably fail again,' she says. The attempt to quit is doomed before it's even begun.

Believing in the Perfect

Paul is faced with two choices. He can accept a place on a training course, but that means selling his flat and going back to renting – just at the time when house prices are taking off. Or he can keep his flat, but turn down the chance of getting up the career ladder. Either choice has a lot going for it, but neither is ideal. But Paul tells himself that there is invariably a perfect solution to everything, and so he spends days turning over the various options in his mind. In the end he is forced into making a decision in a hurry. He's now spending a lot of time worrying about whether he made the right decision, and so wastes a lot of valuable time he could be spending on his training. When he's anxious he eats, so he's already regained much of the weight he lost on a diet last year.

Negative Thinking

Louise has stopped smoking for three weeks. She was very worried about putting on weight, and so has been careful to follow a low-fat, high-starch diet, and to take plenty of exercise. She's done extremely well so far, despite the occasional unplanned bar of chocolate, and missing her swim at the weekend. But she doesn't see it that way. 'I shouldn't have eaten that chocolate' (why not?). 'It's just as well I went swimming today, considering how much I've been eating'. To her credit, she's still stopped, but she certainly isn't making it easy for herself.

Sounds familiar? But does it help? How could Laura, Chris, Caroline, Paul and Louise have rethought the dialogue in their minds? Perhaps Laura would have found it easier if she'd seen from the beginning that it was unrealistic to ban cake from her diet, or if she'd been able to tell herself that the lapse didn't make her a total failure. Chris might have learnt a lot from the way she handled her interview, which would have helped her next time, if only she'd been able to tell herself that some rejections were inevitable and it didn't mean that she didn't stand a chance. And Louise could have rewarded herself for a job well done, instead of chastising herself for simply being human. Just noticing how irrational our thinking can be, and rethinking it can help. It's all too easy to believe that by focusing on our shortcomings we can make ourselves try harder. But feeling guilty may only make us feel worse.

FRIENDS AND FAMILY

Having someone to talk to can help. Few of us nowadays have the support of an extended family around us, and so end up feeling alone with our problems. In this situation friendship can make all the difference.

But friendly support isn't always all it's cracked up to be. In the first place, it's asking for disappointment if you expect everyone to like you, and to give you their support. In the second, the value of support depends on who is giving it, and who is taking it. Your friends and family *can* help you to stop smoking, to stay slim or to get through a host of other problems, but even without meaning to, they can sabotage your every step:

'*Trying* to stop smoking again are we?' (they don't think you'll succeed); 'Go on – have one to keep me company' (the smoker feels threatened by being left on a sinking ship); 'Stopping smoking? – you'll put on weight you know' (you get into an argument and end up smoking because of it); 'Glad you've finally seen sense at last' (anyone would think that they'd quit smoking, not you); 'Not *another* diet' (meaning that there will be another and still another); 'Go on – one piece of cake won't hurt, I made it myself' (blatant emotional blackmail); 'You've done brilliantly to stop smoking – here's a box of chocolates to cheer you up' (why should you need cheering up?).

Being assertive can help, as can keeping a low profile. 'No thanks – I've stopped smoking.' 'Thank you, but I'm watching my weight.' If you're still being pressured, lie! 'I'm not smoking because I've got a sore throat'; 'Thank you, but I'm not very fond of cake,' or 'Thank you, it looks delicious, – but I just can't manage another mouthful'.

Perhaps even more damaging is the type of help which undermines your confidence. It's all too easy, if you really want to help someone over a problem, to go too far, so making them feel that they cannot manage on their own. The friend or partner who becomes party to your efforts, by hiding your cigarettes, or locking away the biscuits, is not really helping as much as you think.

The other side of the equation is you. Some of us feel immensely reassured if we can talk through our problems, while for others, accepting help is an admission of defeat. At the end of the day, the best type of support is the support *you* want. It may be that you just want someone to listen, or to use as a sounding board, or it may be that you'd welcome their advice, even if you decide not to take it in the end. Perhaps you'd rather your family didn't mention the fact that you've quit smoking, or perhaps you'd like them to ask how you're getting on several times a day. Would it help if everyone co-operated by giving you at least one 'smoke-free' room, or would you prefer to accept that it is your decision to quit, and theirs to continue? Perhaps your friends could help by choosing to do things which don't centre around food and smoking, or by not asking you to buy cigarettes, or make snacks for them? If you're in any doubt about what sort of help you want, you might find it useful to rehearse in your own mind how you could best help *them*, if the situation were reversed. Remember that support is mutual, and that you have to help your friends and family to help you. Thanking them for their support is the best way of ensuring that it continues.

When a Friend Is Not Enough

Sometimes you may need extra help. It may be that there simply isn't anyone you feel you could talk to, or that your friends are already overloaded with problems of their own. Equally, you may feel so overwhelmed by stress or depression that you don't know where to start. If you've tried out some of the suggestions in this chapter, or if you don't feel that you can even begin to tackle them, it may be that you need professional help from a counsellor or therapist to get you started. In the first instance I suggest asking your family doctor to point you in the right direction. Failing that, ask for help from one of the organizations listed at the back of this book.

THE BOREDOM FACTOR

Finally – there's what to do about boredom. As we've seen, smoking is not so much a way of filling time as a way of wasting it, but it is the case that quitting can leave you wondering what to do with your time. Much the same problem can dog the efforts of people who want to stay slim. Reading recipes, planning meals, cooking them and eating can take up a lot of time; so, for that matter, does reading diet books and slimming magazines, counting calories and discussing the latest diet! Either way, there's a gap to fill.

Far be it for me to suggest that you should take up a hobby. Personally, I always cringe when I hear people say this, and I can sympathize with the soap opera star who was heard recently to ask how collecting china thimbles was supposed to solve the mid-life blues. The trouble with boredom is that it's a state of mind. You get so bored that you're too bored to think about what else you could do, let alone actually do it! Cigarettes and food are there for the taking, but taking up a hobby takes effort, and you can't start one at half-past eleven in the evening just because there's nothing to watch on the box.

Planning ahead

So it makes sense to think now about how you're going to fill your time. You have to get the ball rolling for yourself. Some of the skills we've looked at in this book are positive time fillers – exercise, relaxation, and friends. So too are all those things you ought to do, but never manage to get round to. 'Little and often' things make sense when you first quit smoking, by way of celebration – a relaxing warm bath, a sauna, a magazine, a decent book. Perhaps there is something you've always wanted to try, but felt you couldn't achieve (hobbies included), or something you've always wanted to buy, but couldn't afford? Stopping smoking is a great confidence builder, and confidence can help you to make the best of your life.

Use this space to make a list of ten things you plan to do or try when you quit smoking.

1.
2.
3.
4.
5.
6.
7.
8.
9.
10.

8

QUITTING SMOKING

'Usually we expect that nature has a master plan.
But what was it that she expected us to do with tobacco?'

Bill Vaughan

By now nine-tenths of the battle is won. You know what you are up against, and what you have to look forward to, and this is better than any stop-smoking aid you could buy. You should also have done much of the groundwork which will enable you to stop smoking without putting on weight. Just to recap, your personal ground work may have involved:

- Planning a few changes to your eating habits (chapter 4 – Smokeless Fuel).
  Deciding on ways of becoming more active (chapter 5 – Burning It Up)
- Boosting your 'wantpower' (chapter 6 – Thinking About Quitting) and
- Practising how to relax and planning new ways of dealing with stress and other problems (chapter 7 – Lifeskills).

All you have to do now is make the break. There is no reason to expect the worst. By no means everyone who stops smoking finds it difficult, even if they have struggled on previous attempts, and people who put off quitting for years and then stop, almost always end up kicking themselves for not doing it earlier.

THE RIGHT FRAME OF MIND

A question which often arises at this point is this: is it best to stop smoking in one go, or to cut down gradually? If you have ever tried cutting down in the past, then you will know the answer. Almost all smokers who succeed in stopping smoking do it in one go (the 'cold turkey' method) and research has shown that they have less difficulty than smokers who try to cut down.

It is not difficult to see why. Faced with a moment of doubt, there is a world of difference between the smoker who has cut down and the smoker who has stopped. If you are still smoking, then it is all too easy to fudge the issue and have 'just one more', and before you know it you are back where you started. On the other hand, if you have stopped, you have to make a conscious decision to break your resolve and while you are thinking about it the urge will probably pass. The best way to get out of a relationship which goes sour is to break it off once and for all.

The other problem with cutting down is that you end up with the worst of both worlds. You start off hoping that you can wean yourself off the cigarettes gradually – but because you never really stop taking the nicotine, your body keeps on demanding a top-up.

You spend all day just waiting to smoke your next cigarette and not being able to get on with anything else until you do. It's a form of slow torture. Because you are still addicted, the longer you wait, the more enjoyable it seems. So – far from weakening your desire to smoke, you end up strengthening it.

I am always worried when I meet a smoker who, having thought this through, still decides that she wants to go about it the gradual way. Probably the main reason why this method is so rarely successful is that the smoker is not really in the right frame of mind to stop smoking in the first place, and so is held back by the fear that life will never again be the same without cigarettes.

Should you stop now, or put it off for a while, until things at home or work are a bit easier? It is reasonable to be a bit apprehensive about the process of actually stopping smoking, so it does make sense to do it at a time which will make it as easy as possible. If you are the sort of smoker who is used to lighting up when you are under stress, then it would be madness to try to quit smoking and move house all in the same week. On the other hand, if you tend to do most of your smoking when you're bored then it could be just the ticket. Then again, there is no point in escapism. One of my mentors, Dr Howard Williams, used to tell a story, the gist of which was that a lot of very wealthy bankers went on a stop smoking cruise in the Med. As they got on to the boat they were frisked for cigarettes and they then spent a blissful fortnight just 'getting away from it all'. As the boat docked, the news broke of an impending crash on the stock market. Need I say more?

136

Some times are better than others, but there is no point in putting it off indefinitely.

The point is this. If you are in the right frame of mind to quit smoking then you will have reached the point where you just can't wait to stop and nothing and nobody is going to stand in your way. You would not have read this book if you did not want to become a slim ex-smoker, and now is your chance to achieve this goal.

If you are in any doubt about whether you should go ahead, then it may be that, deep down, you have not yet convinced yourself that you want to be free of cigarettes for the rest of your life. The question is what to do about it. There is no point in trying to put the whole idea of stopping smoking out of your mind and hoping that it will just go away. Please believe me, it will not. Once smokers start to question the effect of smoking on their health, their lifestyles or the well-being of those around them, they're rarely entirely happy with their smoking again. Sooner or later, you will feel compelled to try to stop smoking. And even if you fail, sooner or later, you will try again. That is, of course, if you haven't left it too late.

On the Disadvantages of Smoking

There is no point in making a half-hearted attempt. Don't keep hoping that you will just wake up with a bad cold and decide that you can't bear to smoke ever again; people who say this happened to them usually turn out to have been working up to it for years. So keep working up to it yourself. It's important to face facts. Most confirmed smokers go out of their way to avoid thinking about the health consequences and other disadvantages of their smoking, like the man who saw in the *Reader's Digest* that cigarettes are bad for you, and had to give up reading the *Reader's Digest*. Confirmed smokers switch over to another station when they are threatened (yes, threatened) by a programme on how to avoid a heart attack, or find any excuse to avoid a health exhibition. At the same time they are positively relieved to hear someone remarking that 'there is no conclusive proof that smoking causes cancer' (even if it was only a spokesman for the tobacco industry), and delighted if they find out that their doctor happens to smoke (not that many of them do). At the back of her mind, the confirmed smoker has a nagging doubt about the consequences of their habit (when did you last volunteer for a chest x-ray?) but probably tends towards believing that the risks are exaggerated.

Meanwhile, continue to boost your 'wantpower'. Start observing non-smokers and smokers in company. Do the non-smokers really look bored and miserable, as if they are missing out on something; do they look stressed and tense – or is it the smokers who seem never to be able to relax? Try talking to a few ex-smokers – not the sort who will give you a lecture – but someone who is sympathetic. Start looking at the cigarette advertisements which in some countries still find their way on to the back of magazines or appear on television under the guise of sports sponsorship – even at the cigarette pack itself. Don't let this social conditioning counteract the real truth about smoking.

You will know when you are ready to quit by the overwhelming feeling of *relief* that you are never again going to have to poison yourself by your own hands, and by the excitement that you are at long last going to break free.

The Last Cigarette

The best thing is to decide on your stop smoking date and then ceremoniously smoke your last ever cigarette. Take your time. As you inhale, think about where the smoke is going, and imagine how it feels to your lungs, heart and blood vessels as you breathe down the fumes. Notice how the smoke coats your teeth and clings to your hair and your clothes. Imagine how it will feel to know that you have broken free from the stranglehold of tobacco. The time when you smoke your last is also the time to deal with all those bits and pieces which are part of the smoker's clutter. You may need to keep a few matches, but disposable lighters and cheap ashtrays can be thrown out. Don't do this with a sense of mourning (what have you got to lose?), but as the welcome end of a phase of your life – like burning your old school books or putting away baggy maternity clothes. Only the treasured lighter or beautiful ashtray need be kept if you have one; in the years to come, you will find it so difficult to believe that you were ever a smoker that you will need something to remind you that it was true.

What to Expect

When people ask me what to expect in the way of withdrawal symptoms, I always hesitate for a moment. Around 1 in 3 people who quit experience almost no symptoms at all. Another 1 in 3 say that they find them mildly irritating – like having a bad cold. Only the minority find them really troublesome. It would be one thing if everyone experienced them, but not everyone does – and you know how it is when someone mentions 'fleas' and you start to itch. Some quitters really feel that they'd rather not know – or at least cross their bridges when they come to them, and if this is the way you feel, you may want to skip the rest of this chapter and move on now to page 147.

On the other hand, forewarned is forearmed, and many people find it is easier to deal with the withdrawal phase of stopping smoking if they know what is happening to them. As I said, not everyone has a problem, but don't feel that you are unlucky if you do. See the withdrawal phase as the time when you are starving the nicotine out of your system once and for all – looked at this way (to borrow from a one-time British Chancellor), 'if it's hurting, then it must be working'.

How Long Do They Last?

Withdrawal symptoms, if they happen to you, are a positive sign that the body is finally recovering from the years of smoking. Just as your body has had to adjust to your smoking in an attempt to combat the poisons, so does it have to readjust now that you've quit. Within 24-48 hours almost all the nicotine will have disappeared from your bloodstream, and it will take just a few more weeks for your body to start functioning normally again without it. The rule of thumb is this: most withdrawal symptoms are at their worst during the first few days of being an ex-smoker and disappear within three to four weeks.

Don't be deterred if you meet someone who tells you that they are still suffering from terrible withdrawal pangs after eight years of stopping smoking – ask them *why* they quit in the first place? Almost always, they will tell you that they stopped because they felt they *had to*, not because they *wanted to*. I know how they feel, because for a long time there was a small part of me that saw myself as a deprived smoker, rather than a willing ex-smoker. I kept on wishing that someone would invent a safe cigarette so that I could start smoking again, until one day it dawned on me that life without cigarettes was actually better than before. Withdrawal symptoms are temporary – and they are a very small price to pay for a lifetime's freedom from smoking.

So – what *can* you expect, and what can you do about it? Here are some common withdrawal symptoms, and some suggestions for beating them. Remember that by no means everyone experiences them, and that very few people experience them all.

A cough shows that the cleaning mechanisms of the lung are recovering from the damage done by smoking and are clearing out the tar and other debris which has built up. Don't be surprised if your smoker's cough gets temporarily worse or if you suddenly develop one out of the blue – this is why. The cough will go in a week or so.

A dizzy or 'high' feeling is due to nicotine withdrawal. If you are really badly affected, don't drive. The feeling disappears very quickly, usually within a day or two. Don't fight it, enjoy it!

Tingling sensations or 'pins and needles' are probably a sign that your heart and circulatory system is recovering. They don't last.

Constipation happens because the bowel has become reliant on nicotine to make it work. If you're eating plenty of high-fibre foods and lots of fruit and vegetables, it shouldn't be a problem. Keep up the fluid intake too – plenty of water and fruit juice (diluted with soda or mineral water, to keep the calories low).

Tiredness and lethargy may occur because of a fall in nervous activity in the brain. Once it has readjusted to the lack of nicotine, activity should return to normal, and in the meantime, taking exercise should help. On the other hand, some quitters experience:

Sleeplessness, which probably reflects the general upheaval in your body when you first quit. It's not uncommon to hear people say that after an initial week of sleeping badly, they then can't stay awake.

Mouth sores and ulcers are a sign that the chemical and bacterial composition of your mouth is recovering from the many irritant chemicals in cigarette smoke. They rarely last. If they persist, seek medical help from your doctor or pharmacist.

Difficulty concentrating is another sign of nicotine withdrawal. It does *not* mean that you will never be able to concentrate again, but a few people do find it frustrating – especially if they are under pressure. Remember that smoking gave you 'time out' – a few moments to sit back and reflect on the problem ahead, so don't leap into a piece of work and then wonder why you can't get your thoughts down.

Try to prioritize and don't do anything you don't have to. Talk to your boss if you think you will get a sympathetic ear. As smokers take twice as much time off work due to sickness as non-smokers, a temporary 'blip' in your work performance should hardly matter. If you do have to press on regardless, don't despair – you'll be surprised at how much you can do when you have to.

Anxiety and tension are also signs of nicotine withdrawal, and they are temporary. They range from mild irritability to wanting to wring someone's neck – but they do *not* mean that you are deep down a nasty, bad-tempered person who will never be able to keep calm. Smoking puts up your heart rate and blood pressure and makes your hands shake: you will be better off without it. Don't let a bad day start you off feeling down about not smoking. There will always be bad days – breaking your resolve won't make them better. If you're having problems, look back over the suggestions in chapters 5 and 7 – go and take your anger out on the pavement or the running track, and put your relaxation skills into practice.

Craving – an empty, or gnawing feeling, or the thought that 'I badly want a cigarette'. No-one knows precisely why it occurs, although some of it is simply due to wanting to get rid of other withdrawal symptoms. The most important thing to know about craving is that it passes. To begin with you may experience it quite frequently, but it becomes less and less frequent, and not nearly as strong, until eventually it disappears all together. Don't fight it. Accept that cravings will come and go. One of the tricks many quitters say they found useful is to think of every craving as a little demon popping up on their shoulder. Instead of panicking and wondering how long they will be able to resist the temptation, they greet the demon with the thought of 'oh, hello – you again'. The challenge is to outwit the demon and starve the nicotine and other poisons out of your system. Deep breathing and relaxing may help (see page 118).

Finally there's **habit**. Taking a cigarette out of its packet, lighting up and smoking is an action which you have probably repeated many times in the same situations. Now that you are no longer smoking, you may also find it helpful as a temporary ploy to avoid some of the cues which trigger a desire to smoke. Some of the most common ones are listed on the next few pages, together with the popular ways of avoiding them. You may want to add your own ideas to the list.

The First Cigarette of the Day

Notice right from day one how nice it is not to wake up feeling groggy from the night before; how much more alert and fresh you feel. Make a point of throwing open the windows if it is fine. Try altering your routine. If you normally linger in bed, get up straightaway, take an invigorating shower, or go for a walk – or set the alarm for later and get some extra rest. Try listening to the radio or breakfast TV for a change, or if you do anyway, tune into a different station.

The After Meal Cigarette

The best bet is to get up from the table as soon as you have finished eating, and do something else; go for a walk, phone a friend, go to a different room or even just a different chair, get on with something, even if it is just the washing up. It will be much easier to resist a second helping if you've planned a filling, satisfying meal – just enough for one helping and no more.

The Telephone Cigarette

If you find this a problem, just stop and think for a second. There is something very wrong if you've reached the point where you can't even make a quick phone call without a cigarette – and how much better would it be if you could manage without. This is a habit which can be broken, even if it's a bit strange at first. Try holding the telephone in the other hand, or doodling with a pencil and paper while you're talking.

The Car Cigarette

If you're used to smoking in the car, reflect on the fact that smokers have one and a half times as many accidents as non-smokers. It's so easy to drop your lighter, or your matches, or a lit cigarette, and while you're trying to prevent a fire you end up having an accident instead. On a cold or wet day when windows are shut, carbon monoxide inside the car can also rise to a level which can seriously impair your judgement.

A car is a good place to create a 'smoke-free' zone.

Give it a good clean out, empty the ashtrays, and put in some air fresheners instead. Try a new radio station or cassette to distract you. If you find yourself swearing at the wheel in a traffic jam, take a few slow deep breaths and try to relax. Smoking doesn't get you there any faster.

The Social Cigarette

How you deal with this depends on who you are with. If you are with people who don't smoke, then you will probably enjoy socializing as much as usual; either you wouldn't have smoked anyway, or you would have been the odd one out, trying to blow your smoke behind you so that it didn't get into their eyes and then getting complaints from the people behind.

If your friends are smokers, don't watch them smoking with envy, but with relief. They may *look* as if they are enjoying their smoking, but the enjoyment of cigarettes is a deadly illusion. Even if they are getting some social pleasure out of sharing their 'poison' it is likely to be short-lived; any day now, they will be wanting to join you. Try to avoid falling into the trap of having a cigarette because you think it will make your friend feel better. She is not smoking just one – she will still be smoking tomorrow, and the next day and the next, and so will you if you join her.

The other thing to watch for is alcohol. There's no need to become a teetotaller. Check the suggestions on page 80.

THE TASTE OF FREEDOM

What does it feel like to be an ex-smoker? Many people who quit smoking recall the moment that they smoked their last cigarette as a turning point in their lives. I must say this has always struck me as rather odd, because the period immediately after stopping smoking is a sort of limbo. On the one hand, you know that you have stopped, you're even quite enjoying it at times, but on the other hand, you can't quite believe it. Then one day you wake up to find yourself in the real world again – looking forward to the future and knowing with certainty that cigarettes don't have to play a part in it. Even if you are still having to *work* at being a non-smoker, you know that you have broken free. It may take a few days, or even a few weeks – but it is a moment well worth waiting for. It's a once-in-a-lifetime experience – the only true advantage of ever having smoked in the first place.

FACING THE FACTS

Being well informed about smoking is one of the keys to boosting your wantpower. A lot of people seriously underestimate the risks. Check out your own knowledge using the questionnaire below. (The answers are at the end of chapter 9.)

1. Smoking just one cigarette makes your heart rate increase and your blood pressure go up.

A. True
B. False

2. How many premature deaths are caused by smoking as compared to traffic accidents, alcohol abuse, drug abuse and suicide?

A. Smoking causes twice as many premature deaths as the total of the other causes
B. The other causes lead to twice as many premature deaths as smoking
C. Smoking causes more than four times as many premature deaths as the total of other causes

3. Women who smoke 25 or more cigarettes a day and also take the pill have an increased risk of a heart attack. Is the risk increased:

A. 3 times
B. 10 times
C. 40 times
D. 100 times

4. Over 95 per cent of people who suffer from arterial disease of the legs (which causes pain on walking and can lead to amputations) are cigarette smokers.

A. True
B. False

5. More than 9 out of every 10 cases of lung cancer occur in people who smoke. Smokers are also much more likely to get which of the following?

Cancer of the mouth
Bronchitis
Cancer of the bladder
Emphysema
Stroke
Cancer of the cervix (in women)
Peptic ulcers

6. You are much less likely to get a smoking-related disease if you smoke low tar cigarettes

A. True
B. False

7. Smoking can make you feel cold.

A. True
B. False

8. A female smoker who smokes 20 cigarettes a day will spend around £14 a week on her smoking. If she quits smoking at the age of 30, and invests the money in an 'endowment with profits' savings plan, how big a lump sum would she expect to receive at age 60? (assuming a cumulative interest rate of just 7 per cent)

A. £20,250
B. £31,500
C. £43,600
D. £55,600

9. Women who smoke are more likely to have painful and irregular periods.

   A. True
   B. False

10. You have to smoke at least 15 cigarettes a day to have a substantially greater risk of dying young than someone who doesn't smoke

   A. True
   B. False

11. Smoking leads to premature facial wrinkling.

   A. True
   B. False

12. From the moment you quit, your body begins to recover from the damage done by smoking.

   A. True
   B. False

9

STAYING STOPPED, STAYING SLIM

There's not a Shakespeare sonnet
or a Beethoven quartet
That's easier to like than you
Or harder to forget.

You think that sounds extravagant
I haven't finished yet
I like you more than I would like
To have a cigarette

'Giving Up Smoking'
by Wendy Cope[1]

The process of stopping smoking is, if not exciting, at least preoccupying. It gives you something to think about. There is a sense of novelty, and you have the feeling of being carried along on the crest of the wave. As the hours, and then the days, and then the weeks, and then the months pass, you will experience a tremendous sense of achievement and self-confidence.

Then one day, the novelty wears off. Sooner or later, you are struck by the fact that you have now joined the two-thirds *majority* of people who choose not to

[1] from her collection *Making Cocoa for Kingsley Amis* (1986), Faber & Faber Ltd, with kind permission

151

smoke. This doesn't make you ordinary – far from it – but it can suddenly feel that way. And it is at this point that many ex-smokers become vulnerable to what a colleague of mine liked to call retrospective nostalgia. They start looking wistfully back on their smoking days and imagining that life then was altogether much easier, or more pleasant than it is now, and wondering whether they could smoke just one cigarette. I call this the rose-tinted glasses syndrome.

There is an uncomfortable parallel here with the psychology of dieting. To start with, there is the challenge of a new diet, special foods to be bought, calories to be counted or units to be juggled, and the excitement of working out how long it will take you to reach your goal. Then there is the thrill of watching the scales register ever lower, the joy of being able to shed old clothes and buy new ones, and the endless round of compliments. But even here, the novelty can wear off. The diet foods become boring, and the dieter starts to dream about places where mountains are made of chocolate ice cream and rivers of hot fudge sauce. There is also the disappointment that slimness does not entirely live up to the promised land which dieters are often led to expect. It is at this point that the newly slimmer dieter becomes vulnerable to breaking her diet, just until tomorrow, next Monday, or next year, just as the ex-smoker becomes vulnerable to smoking 'just one cigarette'.

But here the similarity stops. You need to eat to live. But you do not need to smoke, and on the contrary you are likely to live much longer if you don't. And to my way of thinking, this means that the strategies for staying stopped and staying slim are entirely different. With eating, you have to learn to pat the dragon on the back at least three times a day, and it makes no sense at all to resolve never again to eat this food or that, or never again to eat at certain times or in certain situations. But with smoking it's different. It makes perfect sense to resolve never, ever again to take even so much as a puff of a cigarette and many, many ex-smokers have done precisely this with proven success. But how does it work in practice?

STAYING STOPPED

If I had a pound for every smoker I met who had stopped smoking and gone back to it as a result of smoking 'just one cigarette', I would be a rich woman. I heard about one smoker who had quit smoking for eight months and then smoked 'just one cigarette' on December 31st, so that he'd always be able to say that he'd quit for a New Year's resolution. That was three years before, and that one cigarette had become another and another and another. To begin with he'd cadge just the occasional one from a friend, then he bought a pack of cigarettes so he could pay the friend back, then he bought a pack for himself and before he knew it, he was back where he started. That one cigarette had proved to be a very, very expensive cigarette indeed. It's all too tempting to believe that now that you've stopped you can have the occasional one, but I can count on the thumb of one hand the number of quitters I know who have been able to do this. For most of us, that first cigarette is the beginning of a very slippery slope. Of course, you may already know this from personal experience.

One Cigarette Classics

Why is it then that time and time again people set foot on the slope? Just when the whole smoking issue had begun to fade from memory, they find themselves with a lit cigarette in their hand, and wondering how and why it happened. Typically, there are certain situations which lead people back to smoking that first, fatal cigarette – and they all have in common the element of surprise. But forewarned is forearmed. What you have to do is to *anticipate* the problems, and work out in advance how you will cope with them. The one cigarette classics fall into two groups. The first group includes all general day-to-day situations in which you used to smoke – for example when you were drinking alcohol, or you were under pressure at work or home. Combination situations can prove especially difficult – say when you find yourself alone at home, with not much to do, but with a difficult problem on your mind. It's all too easy to get fixed on the idea that when you smoked you could handle this sort of situation so much better, and before you know it you're smoking again. In reality, there are many reasons why you were more or less able to cope six months or six years ago, but most have nothing whatsoever to do with smoking, and starting again will undoubtedly make the situation worse, not better. We have already looked at a whole range of skills which can help you to cope without smoking. The important thing is to be ready and prepared to use them.

The other group of situations fall into the one-off category. A funeral is a sad, but classic example. So is an unexpected celebration or party, as is a holiday. In fact any situation which you face for the first time since you've stopped smoking, no matter how much time has elapsed, can put you at risk. There is an element of *déjà vu*. The last time you were with your ex-lover, or the last time you were sunbathing on a Greek island, you were smoking a cigarette – and the situation just doesn't seem right without one. And in a moment of sheer madness you imagine that it will be possible to smoke just for today, or just for your holiday, fondly believing that your desire to smoke will disappear as soon as you get off the plane.

Perhaps the most difficult thing about these situations, particularly the sad ones, is that reasoning doesn't always help. In a moment of despair you may not be able to see that smoking will just add to the problem, much less that the long-term disadvantages will far outweigh the hoped for advantage of smoking a cigarette right now.

THE POWER OF SUGGESTION

It is for this reason that I think it's important to work from the very beginning at making not smoking something you do *automatically*. The relevant technique is autosuggestion. Make a point of repeating to yourself as often as possible that you are a non-smoker –

someone who doesn't smoke. If you find it helpful, practise saying it in front of a mirror. The more often you repeat the words, the more you convince yourself that you never, ever want to smoke again, the less likely you are to succumb in a moment of surprise.

Of course, none of this means that if, despite all your efforts, you do find yourself smoking 'just one cigarette' you have to throw in the towel. A return to smoking is not inevitable, unless you make it so in your mind. Make a note of what prompted you to smoke the cigarette, and then set the lapse behind you and carry on. You may have lost a battle, but you haven't lost the war.

Last but not least, never lose sight of what you have achieved by stopping smoking, staying slim or losing weight. Many people find it helpful to mark in some way the date on which they finally packed in their smoking for good, perhaps with a small celebration, or a regular donation to charity. Every year, on January 27th, I receive a beautiful bouquet of flowers from a gentleman who quit smoking in a stop smoking group which I ran some years ago. Touching though the gift is, I am always reminded of the fact that stopping smoking was his achievement, not mine, but in a way, the gift of flowers is as much for him as it is for me. He knows, as only an ex-smoker can know, that not smoking is an achievement worth celebrating.

The same is of course true of being slim. A health promotion officer who I used to meet quite frequently told me that she keeps in her wardrobe a treasured pair of designer jeans which she wears only on special occasions. They serve as a constant reminder to her of the joys of being a slim ex-smoker in a slim world, and she has been known to walk out of a chocolate shop empty-handed just by saying to herself 'French jeans'. I expect that like me she also scours the supermarket shelves for new low-fat varieties of familiar foods, and new recipes, and makes a point of listening to the budget each year, to work out how much money she is saving as the price of cigarettes rises (hopefully) inexorably upwards.

Striking Back

In time, many ex-smokers also come to feel extremely angry about the activities of the tobacco industry, which continues to promote and sell a lethal product in the face of overwhelming evidence as to the consequences. It's not difficult to understand why. Every day, the tobacco industry worldwide must recruit new smokers to replace the many adult smokers who quit smoking by dying. Most of them will be children, perhaps *your* children. Tobacco, remember, is a unique product. It is dangerous when used exactly as the manufacturer intended: remove from packet . . . put in mouth . . . light . . . inhale. The evidence is irrefutable. Tobacco kills.

Yet you would never believe it to look at the advertising, would you? Advertising presents smoking in an acceptable light. It allows you to believe that smoking is an OK thing to do. But it isn't. Why is it that the industry insists that tobacco advertising and sponsorship has no influence on children, its most important market, yet vigorously campaigns to promote its lethal products worldwide? Can it really be just about brand-switching, as the industry implies, can it really be a coincidence that children smoke the most advertised brands, or is it because, in the words of Brendan Brady, spokesman for the Tobacco Advisory Council:

> 'Every industry has to recruit customers. We recruit new customers once they're over the age of 16. Of course they see the advertising before that age; of course, they see people smoking before that age. They make up their – the decisions (sic) before that age. But . . . we're not interested in the market under the age of 16' . . .

The facts about smoking and health have been known for a long, long time. The industry has been given ample time to quit. But it hasn't. Diversification has provided an opportunity for infiltration, and while we in the West have been preoccupied with reducing the death rate due to smoking, the industry has been cynically promoting its products in developing countries, where the appalling consequences of poverty mask the holocaust yet to come. Please don't leave the lobbying to the health profession – we need your help, and with it, we can help to end the epidemic of smoking-related disease and death.

There Is No Such Thing As Failure

I would like to end, where I began, on a personal note. During the years when I was struggling to stop smoking and lose weight, I did as you have done, and bought and read books which I hoped would provide The Answer. Like this book, most were written by someone who had successfully overcome the problem in hand, and not infrequently they carried glowing 'before and after' testimonials. I would read the book, try the method, but it just didn't work for me. I became depressed. If the author could do it, why couldn't I? And the harder I tried, the more I failed.

So what if you have read this book from cover to cover, but it hasn't worked for you? Does this mean that you need to buy another book, try another method, or a new kind of diet? What about all those various stop smoking tablets and aids, or hypnotism or acupuncture? Would they help? The answer is probably yes and no. Yes, most stop smoking aids can be helpful at least to some people, some of the time, but no, none of them is a substitute for a firm and reasoned decision, that what you want to do is stop smoking more than you want to continue. They are aids, not miracle cures.

I should perhaps mention, in passing, nicotine replacement, the one stop smoking therapy which has been shown to limit weight gain in quitters. This makes it particularly relevant to the problem in hand. Nicotine replacement is currently available in the UK and elsewhere as nicotine chewing gum, and over the next few years we can expect to see the introduction of other products, such as the nicotine patch, now available on prescription. The idea is to help you break the smoking habit in two stages. In the first, you get used to not smoking, while still taking in some nicotine to help keep withdrawal symptoms at bay. In the second, you eliminate the nicotine as well. Not surprisingly, the therapy is helpful at least to some quitters, although it is most effective when combined with advice and counselling. As for its effects on weight gain, research trials have generally shown that smokers who take nicotine during quitting gain less weight than smokers who don't.

But there are grounds for caution. First, the effect of the therapy on weight gain was small, just a few pounds. Second, the main effect seemed to be to delay weight gain, rather than prevent it – in one study, quitters who stopped taking the nicotine almost caught up in weight with the controls (those who had never taken it). The third problem is that some people who succeed in stopping smoking with the gum also become addicted to it. Of course, taking nicotine is very much less dangerous than smoking cigarettes, but opinion is divided as to whether it is entirely safe. My advice is to use nicotine replacement therapy only as a last resort. After all, one of the greatest joys which comes of stopping smoking is the knowledge that you are able to take control of your own life.

Perseverance Pays Off

You will realize from this that I don't believe that failure to quit smoking, lose weight or stay slim is caused by choosing the wrong book, or the wrong approach. The problem, I suspect, is actually one of timing and circumstances. This does not mean that you will never be able to reach your goal, if you really want to. On the contrary, very few people who buy a book like this achieve instant success. For the most part, it's a question of reading, absorbing and thinking and then acting when the circumstances come right.

Nor do I want to blow my own trumpet. I would be the first to admit that there have been a lot of factors involved in helping me to stop smoking and lose weight, other than my own personal effort. Working in a medical school helped to bring home to me the consequences of smoking and so encouraged me to stop smoking and stay stopped. I have had interesting jobs and plenty to think about, and I've been able to reorganize my life so that it doesn't revolve around eating, drinking and smoking. On the other hand, I doubt if I would ever have succeeded if I had not, over the years, read and thought a great deal about stopping smoking and losing weight, and thought about where I was going wrong, and how I could tackle the problem next time.

Perhaps what I'm really saying is that fortune favours the well-prepared. Every effort you make takes you one step closer to your goal of becoming a slim ex-smoker. And if at first you don't succeed, be prepared to try, try and try again. In the meantime, the important thing is to live every day to the full. I would like to wish you health and happiness, and all the very best which life has to offer.

FACING THE FACTS (ANSWERS TO QUESTIONNAIRE ON PAGE 147)

1 A. Smoking *just one* cigarette can increase your heart rate and blood pressure. Regular smoking puts an enormous strain on the heart.

2 A. Four times as many premature deaths are caused by smoking as by traffic accidents, alcohol abuse, drug abuse and suicide combined.

3 C. Women who smoke 25 or more cigarettes a day and also take the pill have 40 times the risk of a heart attack of non-smoking, non-pill takers. The risk in non-smokers who take the pill is virtually negligible, particularly if they use it for less than ten years.

4 A. Over 95 per cent of people who suffer from arterial disease of the legs are cigarette smokers. One rare form of peripheral vascular disease is Buerger's syndrome, which often leads to multiple amputations. It is virtually always due to heavy smoking.

5 All of them. Smoking is a causative agent in cancers of the mouth, throat and oesophagus and pancreas, it is a contributory factor in cancers of the bladder and kidney. Smoking is a risk factor for cancer of the cervix, probably because it depresses the body's ability to cope with infections. Smoking is also the major cause of Chronic Obstructive Lung Disease (including bronchitis and emphysema), which accounts for ¼ of smoking-related deaths. Emphysema involves the progressive destruction of the air sacs in the lung, so reducing the surface area available to absorb oxygen. Emphysema is a crippling disease and it is irreversible.

6 B. Low tar cigarettes are also often low in nicotine, the addictive chemical which keeps people smoking. People who switch from high tar to low tar cigarettes often end up smoking more of them, or without realizing it, inhale more often or more deeply so as to keep nicotine levels up. Smoking low tar cigarettes may slightly reduce the risk of lung cancer, but has no effect on the risk of a heart attack, which accounts for roughly the same number of smoking-related deaths. The current practice of advertising cigarettes as 'low', 'lower' and 'lowest' plays upon the fears of smokers who are worried about their health. The only safe cigarette is an unlit one.

7 A. Smoking can make you feel cold, because it restricts blood flow to the periphery – hands and feet for example.

8 D. A woman who quits smoking twenty cigarettes a day at age 30, and invests the money saved in an 'endowment with profits' saving plan, can expect to receive a lump sum payment at the age of 60 of between £55,600 and £104,000. If the price of cigarettes rises faster than inflation, and she continues to invest the current cost of a week's smoking into the plan, her eventual lump sum would be worth even more in real terms. (Figures based on Sun Alliance Insurance Group, January 1992, assuming cumulative interest rates of between 7 and 10.5 per cent).

9. A. A survey carried out among nearly 3000 women living in England found that smokers were more likely to suffer from more heavy, painful or irregular periods than non-smokers. This may be because smoking interferes with the levels of reproductive hormones.

10 B. The excess risk of smoking-related disease is evident even in people who smoke only a few cigarettes daily. One study found that nurses who smoked just 1-4 cigarettes a day were twice as likely to suffer a heart attack as nurses who didn't smoke.

11 A. A recent study in the USA has put paid to the controversy as to whether smoking is or is not associated with premature wrinkling. After taking into account the influence of age, sex and sun exposure, the researchers found that smoking did lead to premature wrinkling. Heavy smokers were almost five times more likely to be wrinkled as non-smokers. Sun exposure also increased the chances of being wrinkled and the combination of the two was worse than the sum of two separate risk factors combined.

12 A. From the moment you quit, your body begins to recover from the damage done by smoking. You may find that you are able to breathe more easily, or that you generally feel fitter and healthier. Even if you do not experience any of these changes, your long-term risk of disease starts to fall immediately. In general, smokers who quit before the age of 50 halve their risk of dying in the next 15 years, compared with people who carry on. The younger you quit the better, but some benefit applies at every age. No matter how old you are or how long you have been smoking, you stand to improve your chances of living a longer and healthier life by quitting.

APPENDIX:
WHERE TO FIND HELP

Here is a list of the main non-commercial organizations which can help with stopping smoking. Some provide leaflets, some run stop smoking groups and counselling services, some will be able to refer you to local sources of help with stopping smoking (including complementary therapies) and related problems (such as overeating or stress). There are also several commercial outfits. Costs vary, but can be prohibitive.

In the UK

Help should be available from your GP, and you should check to see whether the practice runs stop smoking groups or other services. For specialist information contact:

ASH – Action On Smoking and Health, 109 Gloucester Place, London, W1H 3PH. Tel: 071 935 3519

ASH in Scotland, 8 Frederick Street, Edinburgh, EH2 2HB. Tel: 031 225 4725

ASH in Wales, 142 Whitchurch Rd, Cardiff, CF4 3NA. Tel: 0222 614399

ASH Northern Ireland & Ulster Cancer Foundation, 40 Eglantine Avenue, Belfast, BT9 6DX. Tel: 0232 663281

Glasgow 2000, 20 Cochrane St, Glasgow, G1 1HL. Tel: 041 227 4438

Local Health Promotion/Education Centres:
Look for the address and telephone number under 'Health Authority' in the phone book, or contact in England: The Health Education Authority, Hamilton House, Mabledon Place, London WC1H 9TX (tel: 071 383 3833); in Scotland: The Health Education Board for Scotland, Health Education Centre, Woodburn House, Canaan Lane, Edinburgh, EH10 4SG (tel: 031 447 8044); in Wales: Health Promotion Authority for Wales, 8th Floor, Brunel House, 2 Fitzalan Rd, Cardiff, CF2 1EB (tel: 0222 472472); or in Northern Ireland: The Health Promotion Agency for Northern Ireland, 'The Beeches', 12 Hampton Manor Drive, Belfast, BT7 3EN (tel: 0232 644811)

QUIT & The Smokers' Quitline, 102 Gloucester Place, London, W1H 3DA. Tel: 071 487 2858 (General Office)
Tel: 071 487 3000 (Quitline – a national telephone counselling and referral service).

No Smoking Day:
A national campaign to help smokers who want to stop, run annually on the second Wednesday in March. For information on local activities, contact your local health promotion unit, see above.

Smokestop, Department of Psychology, University of Southampton, Southampton, SO9 5NH. Tel: 0703 583741/592327

Stop Smoking, PO Box 100, Plymouth, Devon, PL1 1RG. Tel: 0752 709506

In the USA

The following headquarters offices of national charities will be able to refer you to your local branch for information about cessation services in your area. Don't forget to ask for help from your physician too.

The American Lung Association, 1740 The Broadway, New York, NY 10019-4374. Phone: (212) 315-8700

The American Heart Association, 7320 Greenville Ave, Dallas, Texas 75231. Phone: (214) 750 5300

The American Cancer Society, Travel 7, Third Avenue, New York, NY 10017. Phone: (010) 212 7363030

The Seventh Day Adventists, General Conference, 12501 Old Columbia Pike, Silver Spring, Maryland 20904. Phone: (301) 680 6000

In Australia

The following offices should be able to refer you to local information on stop smoking services. Help may also be available from your general practitioner, your local community health centres and health promotion units.

ACT Cancer Society Inc, 15 Theodore St, Curtin ACT
PO Box 316, Curtin ACT 2605
Phone: (06) 285 3070
(06) 285 3452 (Quitline)

NSW State Cancer Council, 500 George Street, Sydney NSW 2000
P.O Box 7070, Sydney NSW 2001

Phone: (02) 264 9335
008 177 833 (toll free)

Queensland Cancer Fund, 553 Gregory Terrace, Fortitude Valley 4006
PO Box 201, Spring Hill Q 4004
Phone: (07) 257 1155

South Australian Smoking and Health Project, Anti-Cancer Foundation, 24 Brougham Place, North Adelaide 5006
Phone: (081) 267 5222
(08) 11538 (Quitline)
(08) 267 1833 (Quit Advisory Service)

The Victorian Smoking & Health Program, The Quit Campaign, 12 Victoria Street (PO Box 888), Carlton South 3053
Phone: (03) 663 7777 (Tips & Information)
(03) 11538 (Quitline)
(03) 482 2711 (counselling)

The NT Anti-Cancer Foundation Inc., Shop 24 Ground Floor, Casuarina Plaza, Casuarina N.T. 0810
Tel: (089) 27 4888

Department of Health & Community Services, PO Box 40596, Casuarina NT 0811
Phone: (089) 27 4888

Western Australian Health Department, Health Promotion Services Branch, Ground Floor, C Block, 189 Royal Street, East Perth WA 6004
PO Box 8172, Stirling St PO, Perth WA 6849
Phone: (09) 222 2063

National Heart Foundation, National Office, PO Box 2, Woden ACT 2606
Phone: (06) 282 2144

The Adventist Health Department, 84 The Boulevard, Strathfield, NSW 2135
Phone: (02) 747 5655

In New Zealand

Help may also be available from your family doctor, area health board, hospital or public health nurse.

ASH – Action on Smoking and Health, Rms 24-27 Islington Block, Auckland Hospital, 2 Park Rd, Grafton
P.O. Box 8667, Symonds St, Auckland
Phone: (09) 309 9360
(09) 309 8676

The Auckland Asthma Society, PO Box 67066, Mount Eden, Auckland 3

The Cancer Society of New Zealand Inc., PO Box 1724, Auckland
Phone: (09) 534 0023

The National Heart Foundation, 17 Great South Road, Newmarket
PO Box 17-160, Greenlane, Auckland 5
Phone: (09) 524 6005

Seventh Day Adventists, 743 Great South Rd, Manakau City
Phone: (09) 267 5540
36 Bealey Avenue, Christchurch
Phone: (03) 62 899

SOS – Stop Ourselves Smoking
Phone: (09) 601 999 (Central Auckland)
(09) 837 2777 (West Auckland)
(09) 277 9660 (South Auckland)

In South Africa

The Council Against Smoking, PO Box 23244, Joubertpark 2044
 Phone: 011-6432958
Smokenders, PO Box 41753, Craighall 2024
 Phone: 011-7894483
Breath Free Programme, Seventh Day Adventist Church, 165 Main Road, Somerset West 7130
 Phone: 024 21140

Thanks to the organizations who generously provided the information from which I compiled this list.

INDEX

Also available . . .

KICK IT!
Stop Smoking in 5 Days

JUDY PERLMUTTER

This is the most successful stop-smoking plan ever devised. Judy Perlmutter's Habit Breakers Clinic in America has an 80% success rate a whole year after treatment – incredible when you compare this with the 25% to 35% success rates of other popular stop-smoking methods.

KICK IT! is a proven step-by-step plan based on research and the experiences of people who have tried to give up. So confident is the author of her system that we give a guarantee: quit smoking using this book or your money back.

In this book Judy Perlmutter shares her trade secrets so you no longer have any excuse!

- Guides you effortlessly through each stage of the five-day programme
- Reveals what to do if you feel yourself giving in to temptation
- Explains how to give up on your own or with someone else
- Motivates you to give up for good

KICK IT!	0 7225 1523 5	£3.50	☐
FLATTEN YOUR STOMACH FOR WOMEN	0 7225 1857 9	£3.99	☐
FLATTEN YOUR STOMACH FOR MEN	0 7225 1936 2	£3.99	☐
FULLY FIT IN 60 MINUTES A WEEK — WOMEN	0 7225 1848 X	£2.99	☐
FULLY FIT IN 60 MINUTES A WEEK — MEN	0 7225 1847 1	£2.99	☐
HOW TO BANISH CELLULITE FOREVER	0 7225 2708 X	£3.99	☐
ONCE A WEEK FITNESS FOR WOMEN	0 7225 1892 7	£2.50	☐
SLIMMING YOUR HIPS AND THIGHS	0 7225 1856 0	£2.99	☐

All these books are available from your local bookseller or can be ordered direct from the publishers.

To order direct just tick the titles you want and fill in the form below:

Name: _____

Address: _____

_____

_____ Postcode: _____

Send to: Thorsons Mail Order, Dept 3, HarperCollins*Publishers*, Westerhill Road, Bishopbriggs, Glasgow G64 2QT.
Please enclose a cheque or postal order or your authority to debit your Visa/Access account —

Credit card no: _____

Expiry date: _____

Signature: _____

— up to the value of the cover price plus:
UK & BFPO: Add £1.00 for the first book and 25p for each additional book ordered.
Overseas orders including Eire: Please add £2.95 service charge. Books will be sent by surface mail but quotes for airmail despatches will be given on request.

24 HOUR TELEPHONE ORDERING SERVICE FOR ACCESS/ VISA CARDHOLDERS — TEL: **041 772 2281.**